Iconography:
An Irreverent Introduction

Ángel Rafael Colón
and
Patricia Ann Colón

ISBN: 978-0-692-80704-0

Published by Ingram Book Group, Inc., LaVergne, TN 37086

Library of Congress Cataloging-in-Publication Data

Iconography: An Irreverent Introduction includes figures, appendix of
tables, bibliographic references and index. Chapters and keywords are 1.
Religious Iconography. 2. Mythology and Allegory. 3. Dutch
Iconography. 4. Erratic or miscellaneous iconography. 5. Death
Iconography (redacted from a thesis submitted to the State University of
California, Dominguez Hills). Tables 1-7 are compiled lastly in the
appendix.

Thanks to Patricia Gamon, PhD

Other books

Nurturing Children: A History of Pediatrics.
A History of Children: A Socio-Cultural Survey
  Across Millennia
The Boke of Children
The Child in the Iconography of Death
Tincture of Time: A Concise History of Medicine

Pediatric Pathophysiology
Textbook of Pediatric Hepatology
An Outline of Pediatric Hepatology
El Niño Icterico

Covers

Front cover: *Leda and the Swan* by Albert-Ernest Carrier-Belleuse (1824-1887) terracotta c. 1870, Metropolitan Museum of Art, NYC. Back cover: Relief of a phallus with the inscription *hic habitas felicitas* (here lives the happiness). Anonymous, c. 1st century CE, painted travertine from Campania. National Archaeological Museum, Naples. A *Sheela na gig* corbel from the Romanesque-Norman Church of St. Mary and St David, Kilpeck in Herefordshire, c. 1140. Both images are courtesy of Wikimedia Commons and are discussed in Chapter Four, entitled Iconographic Erratics.

The cover design is by St. John William Colón

iii

Unless otherwise noted, all images are in the public domain.
Image sources: AP – photograph by the author
GAP – Google art project
GFDL – Gnu free documentation license
PH – Publications on Art History
WGA – Web gallery of art
WC – Wikimedia Commons

Figures

Front cover: *Leda and the Swan.* Terracotta by Albert-Ernest Carrier-Belleuse. MMA, NYC. Art Resource. WC. Back cover: Anon. *Hic habitas felicitas.* Relief sign outside a Pompeii bakery, 1ˢᵗ century CE, National Archaeological Museum, Naples. Photo by Wolfgang Sauber, GFDL. Anon. *Sheela na gig* corbel from the Romanesque-Norman Church of St Mary & St David, Kilpeck, Herefordshire. Nessy-Pic WC.

1. Giovanni Bellini. *Sacra Conversazione.* Church of San Zaccaria, Venice. AP.
2. Gentile da Fabriano. *Madonna col Bambino tra i santi Nicola di Bari,Caterina d'Alessandria e un donatore.* Staatlichs Museen, Berlin. WC.
3. Andrea di Bartolo. *Madonna and Child with Four Evangelists.* Walters Museum, Baltimore. WC.
4. Lorenzo Lippi. *St. Agatha.* Blanton Museum, Austin Texas. WC.
5. Anon. *St. Lawrence Martyr.* Museum of Fine Arts, Lyon. Photo Marie-Lan Nguyen. WC.
6. Anon. *St. Dominic.* Wall sculpture on a street in Valletta, Malta. Photo by Marie-Lan Nyguen. WC.
7. Michelangelo Buonarroti. *Last Judgment* (detail). Sistine Chapel, the Vatican. WC.
8. Albert Cornelis. *Mary Magdalene in a Landscape.* National Gallery, London. Photo by Paul Hermans. WC.
9. Lorenzo Lotto. *Madonna with Peter Martyr and John the Baptist.* Museo di Capodimonte, Naples, Italy. WC.
10. Anon. *St. Denis.* Left portal of Notre Dame, Paris. Photo author Anne97432. GFDL. WC.
11. Anon. Tomb slab, Catacomb Domitilla, Rome. 3rd cent. CE. WC.
12. Anon. *Ship Model.* Storkyrkan. Stockholm, Sweden. WC.
13. Bartolomeo di Fruosino. *Desco da Parto.* Metropolitan Museum of Art, New York. Photo by Sarko. WC.
14. Anon. *Square nimbus of Pope John VII.* Mosaic detail. Vatican Museum. GAP.

39. John Stanhope. *Orpheus and Eurydice on the banks of the Styx.* WC.
40. Anthony van Dyke. *Daedalus and Icarus.* Art Gallery of Ontario. WC.
41. Phidias copy. *The Wounded Amazon.* Capitoline Museum, Rome. Photo by Rosemania. WC.
42. Antonio Canova. *Theseus and the Minotaur.* V&A Museum, London. Photo by Yair Haklai. GFDL. WC.
43. Charles-André van Loo. *Perseus and Andromeda.* Hermitage, St. Petersburg. WC.
44. Jean-Leon Gerome. *Pygmalion and Galatea.* MMA, NY. Photo by Imadeo. WC.
45. Gian Lorenzo Bernini. *The Abduction of Prosperine.* Galleria Borghese, Rome. WC.
46. Peter Paul Rubens and Frans Snyders. *Prometheus.* Philadelphia Museum of Art. Photo by Jean-Pol Grandmont. WC.
47. Nicolas Poussin. *Midas and Bacchus.* Alte Pinakothek, Munich. WC.
48. Francois Gérard. *Psyché et l'Amour.* Louvre, Paris. Photo by Sammyday. WC.
49. William Rinehart. *Latona and her Children.* MMA, NY. Photo by Merkens. WC.
50. Joachim Wtewael. *Adonis and Aphrodite.* Hottenbuchau Collection on permanent loan to Liechtenstein, Vienna. WC.
51. Nicolas Bertin. *Phaéton on the Chariot of Apollo.* Louvre, Paris. WC.
52. Paolo Veronese. *Apollo and Daphne.* San Diego Museum of Art. Photo WmPearl. WC.
53. John William Waterhouse. *The Danaides.* PD-Art photographs. WC.
54. Ubaldo Gandolfi. *Selene and Endymion.* LACMA, California. WC.
55. Johann König. *The Death of Niobe's Children.* WGA. WC.
56. Herbert James Draper. *Alcyone seeks her husband.* Artrenewal.org. WC.
57. Paolo Veronese. *Arachne.* Palozzo Ducale, Venice. WC.
58. Pan painter. *Idas and Marpessa separated by Zeus.* Attic-red psykter, Agrigento. Staatliche Antiken Sammlungen, Munich. WC.
59. Anon. *The Naming of Athens.* Model of Parthenon West Pediment (detail) after K. Schwerzek. WC.
60. Hendrik Goltzius. *Cadmus slays the Dragon.* Museet på Koldinghus. National Gallery of Denmark. WC.
61. Tiziano Vecellio (Titian). *Sisyphus.* Prado, Madrid. WC.
62. Gioacchino Assereto. *Tantalus.* Auckland Gallery of Art, NZ. WC.
63. Giovanni Battista Tiepolo. *Bellerophon and Pegasus.* Fresco Palazzo Labia, Venice. WC.
64. Evelyn de Morgan. *Cassandra.* Flickr image. WC.

115. Raphael Sanzio. *The School of Athens* (detail). Sistine Chapel, Vatican. WC.
116. Han Holbein younger. *The Ambassadors.* NGA, London. WGA. WC.
117. William Hogarth. *Gin Lane.* WC.
118. Jean Geoffroy. *La Goutte de Lait de Belleville.* Musée de Assistance Publique, Paris. AP.
119. Francisco Goya. *El Tres de Mayo.* Prado, Madrid. GAP. WC.
120. Eugène Delacroix. *La Liberté Guidant le Peuple.* Louvre, Paris. WC.
121. Pablo Picasso. *Guernica.* © 2017 Estate of Pablo Picasso / Artists Rights Society (ARS), New York.
122. Francisco Goya. *Que Viene el Coco.* Prado, Madrid. WC.
123. Francisco Goya. *El Sueño de la Razón.* Prado, Madrid. WC.
124. Edvard Munch. *The Scream.* Munch Museum, Oslo. GAP. WC.
125. Giorgio Barbarelli da Castelfranco (Giorgione). *The Tempest.* Accademia. Venice. WGA. WC.
126. Éduard Manet. *The Luncheon on the Grass.* Musée d'Orsay, Paris. GAP. WC.
127. John Singer Sargent. *The Daughters of Edward D. Boit.* MFA, Boston (gift of the Boit sisters in honor of Edward Boit). WC.
128. Francesco Salviati. *The Three Fates.* Pitti Palace, Firenzi. WGA. WC.
129. Anon. *Roman Sarcophagus with Prometheus and the Morai.* Louvre, Paris. Photo Jastrow. WC.
130. Gela painter. *Black Figure Pinax Prothesis.* Walters, Baltimore. WC.
131. Anon. *Child Sarcophagus with Conclamatio.* Archeology Museum, Agrigento. AP.
132. Anon. *Child Sarcophagus with Conclamatio.* Cluny, Paris. AP.
133. Anon. *Etruscan Cinerary Lid.* Louvre, Paris. AP.
134. Sabouroff painter. *Lekythos with Charon and Hermes.* Antikensammlung, Berlin. Photo Marcus Byron. WC.
135. Thanatos painter. *Lekythos with Hypnos and Thanatos and Sarpédon.* British Museum. The Yorck Project. WC.
136. Anon. *Four Seasons Sarcophagus with Doorway.* Capitoline Museum, Rome. Photo Jean-Pol Grandmont. WC.
137. Hans Memling. *The Last Judgment.* National Museum of Gdánsk. Photo Aiwaznet.WC.
138. Michelangelo Buonarroti. *Last Judgment* (detail). Sistine Chapel, the Vatican. WC.
139. Anon. *Stele for Apollonia.* Getty Museum. GFDL. WC.

140. Anon. *Maiden holding a Dove.* Archeological Museum Thessaloniki, Greece. Photo Tilemahos Efthimiadia. WC.
141. Anon. *Syrian Boy.* British Museum, London. AP.
142. Anon. *Bibliographical sarcophagus of a Child.* Louvre, Paris. AP.
143. Anon. *Family Grave Marker.* Museo Capitolio, Rome. AP.
144. Anon. *Gisant tombeau des Bartarnay.* Montrésor, Loire Valley, France. Photo Arcyon 37. WC.
145. Germain Pilon. *Tombeau Valentine Balbiari with breviary.* Louvre, Paris. Photo Jebulon, WC.
146. Anon. *Fürst der Welt.* St. Sebaldus Church, Nürnberg. www.sebalduskyrche.de
147. Anon. *Fürst der Welt.* Munster Cathedral, Strasbourg. Photo Albin Denooz. GFDL.WC.
148. Anon. *Fürst der Welt*, Worms Cathedral, Worms. Photo Jivee Blau. WC.
149. Ligier Richier. *Tomb of Rene of Chalon, Prince of Orange.* Church of St. Etienne, Bar-de-Luc, France. Photo Mossot. WC.
150. Germain Pilon. *Tombeau de Henri II et Catherine Medici.* St. Denis, Paris. AP.
151. Anon. *John Fitzalan, Earl of Arundel.* Fitzalan Chapel, Arundel West Sussex. Photo Lampman. WC.
152. Gil de Ronza. *La Muerte.* Museo Nacional de Escultura, Valladolid, Spain. Photo Luis Fernandez Garcia. WC.
153. Anon. *Entrance to St. Olaf's Chapel*, Amsterdam. AP.
154. Jacob van Campen. *Ceremonial Office.* Royal Palace Amsterdam. AP.
155. Stephen Kalcar and Vesalius. *De humanis corpora fabrica.* WC.
156. Adriaen van Utrecht. *Still Life.* WGA. WC.
157. Hans Baldung Grien. *Death and the Maiden.* Kunstmuseum, Basel. WGA. WC.
158. Niklaus Manuel Deutsch. *Mors Osculi.* Kunstmuseum, Basel. Yorck Project. WC.
159. Hans Baldung Grien. *Death and the Maiden.* Kunsthistoriches Musuem, Vienna. PD Art Photograph.WC.
160. C. Alann Gilbert. *All is Vanity.* WC.
161. Anon. *The Three Living and Three Dead.* 15th Century psalter. WC.
162. Holbein the Younger. *Todtentanz.* Project Gutenberg.
163. Bernt Notke. *Danse Macabre* (detail). St. Nicolas Church, Tallinn, Estonia. Cultural Heritage 1255. WC.
164. Rohan master. *Book of Hours.* Spiritualite2000.com/art/enluminures. WC.
165. Anon. *Hyena.* Aberdeen Bestiary 12th century. WC.

189. Anon. *De Wikkelkinderen*. Muiderslot, Muiden, Netherlands. Upload Mandesuka. WC.
190. Anon. *Jan Gerritsz.Pan Family*. Stichting Verzameling Museum. Amsterdam. PH.
191. Jan Jansz.deStomme. *The children of Tjarda van Strachenborch*. Groninger Museum. Groningen, Netherlands. PH.
192. Johann Weidner. *Carl Gustaf Göransson Ulfsparre*. National Museum, Stockholm, Sweden
193. Jansz.de Stomme. *Dead child with wreath*. Groninger Museum, Groningen,Netherlands. Photo Ben Hartman.WC.
194. Nicholas Maes. *George de Vicq as Ganymede*. Fogg Art Museum, Harvard. PH.
195. Johannes Thopas. *Girl on Deathbed*. Royal Picture Gallery. Mauritshuis, The Hague. WC.
196. Bartolomeus van der Helst. *Portrait of a Dead Infant*. Stedelijk Museum, Gouda, Netherlands. PH.
197. Anon. *Gottfried von Schwendi*. St. Stephan Parish Church, Schwendi, Germany. Photo Andreas Praefcke. WC.
198. William Dobson. *Portrait of a Family*. Yale Center for British Art. GAP. WC.
199. Elizabeth Vigée le Brun. *Marie Antoinette and her children* Versailles. Jaconde database. WC.
200. Charles Wilson Peale. *Rachel Weeping*. Philadelphia Museum of Art. WC.
201. William Hogarth. *The Graham Children*. NGA, London. WC.
202. Anon. *Dead Victorian Child*. Glass wet collodion (1875). National Library of Wales. WC.
203. Silvestro dell'Aquila. *Tomb of Maria Pereira*. San Bernadino, Aquila. WGA. WC.
204. Thomas Banks. *Penelope Boothby*. St. Oswald Church, Ashbourne. Photo Eirian Evans. WC.
205. Francis Chantrey. *The Sleeping Children*. Lichfield Cathedral, Staffordshire. WC.
206. Francis Chantrey. *The Stanhope Monument*. Chevening Church, Kent. WC.
207. William Rinehart. *Sleeping Children*. Yale Museum of Art. AP.
208. Anon. St. Brélade, Jersey Island. Photo Man Vyi. WC.

Table of Contents

The first virtue of painting is to be a feast for the eyes.

Eugène Delacroix (1798-1893) in *Journal 1893*

Introduction

This is a book about the pleasures of looking at art – murals, frescoes, mosaics, vases, sculpture and, especially, paintings – of teasing out all the elements of the works; composition, colors, representation, narrative and all the oblique references artists incorporated into their works, commonly as symbols.

This is in fact a book about those symbols, about iconography – arcane visuals that were once universally understood by all viewers. The puzzlement we often felt when standing before a painting unable to fully interpret the opus launched our study of the iconography of art which has been integral to communication from ancient tombstones and sarcophagi to contemporary text messaging.* We are inclined to begin with the 4th century and continue through the 19th centuries. Giorgio Varsari (1511-1574) dabbled a bit in the study of symbols, but only in the 19th century did iconology become a discipline of formal study, in part because by then most had forgotten the meanings of the symbols imbedded in art. Its study, especially during the 20th century, greatly contributed to understanding art in past centuries and thereby enhancing enjoyment of it. Our favorite works in this regard are *Religious Art in France of the Thirteenth Century* by Emile Mâle (1862-1954) and *Studies in Iconology* by Erwin Panofsky (1892-1968).

*Greek and Roman death iconography will be addressed in the last chapter, but the dictionary of texting symbols will not be touched at all. OMG, ATM, LOL & HAND. ☺

Lamentably, the study of iconography evolved into a stuffy, esoteric approach to art with rigid classification and coding systems that drive iconographers into frenzied glossolalia. The iconoclass system, a Dutch innovation, has 28,000 classification types, and 14,000 keywords (closely resembling Chinese complexity but without the benefit of at least learning a language). It is no fun. Iconoclasses don't contribute to the joy of art, but we'll acknowledge they are useful at times as we shall see. In almost all instances, this book will look at art and their symbols without codes, numbers, letters or reference footnotes. (Well, unavoidably, there will be a few – but ignore them, if you like). *En passant*, if you want to learn about paintings that go well with your sofa – don't bother to look here. The intent of this book is to help the viewer appreciate the intellectual as well as aesthetic joys of the old masters by explicating the symbols they used. A penultimate note: this book has a definite Eurocentric focus, and there will be no references to installations, earthworks, neon-tubes, dead animals, urine-pots, TV monitors, funhouse mirrors, curly spiky glass, tarpaulin covered skyscrapers and interactive stuff.

Finally, all the images in this manuscript are in the public domain and were downloaded from the internet to facilitate the reader who would like to view online any particular image in enhanced color and in a larger size. Check the sources listed in the table of figures, such as Wikimedia commons, or Google Art Project. Also, we have a tad of kenophobia, so you will find sporadic gray boxes with "factoid fillers." We use iconography interchangeably with iconology and you will note the occasional bit of neologizing, such as "iconographs," "googleable."

Painting is silent poetry and poetry is painting with words.

Simonides (516-468 BCE) quoted by
Plutarch in *De gloria Atheniensium*

PREFACE

It has been more than fifty years since we began our pilgrimages to art museums all over the world. When we pass through the portals of great art museums, we tend to begin with a visit to the Greek and Roman. Shuffling along, we give due homage to the sculptures, especially the breathtaking statues of Praxiteles, Lysippus and Phidias, the Greek originals and Roman copies. We meander through the Mesopotamian and Etruscan stuff, go past Egyptian mummies and sarcophagi before entering the medieval galleries, where we tend to linger and study specific works, looking for aspects of paintings we may have on prior visits missed. The Medieval is an overture to an exploration of the glories of the Renaissance before the intoxicating pleasure of seeing again the Golden Age of 17th century Dutch art. With several visits in mind, we have the luxury to dawdle and engage.

One of the aspects of art that most interests us, apart from the main subject of a work, is all of the paraphernalia artists throw in. By that we mean artifacts that do not appear to be related to the major theme at all, but in fact are integral and essential to fully comprehend what the artist intended and achieved. They are the elements of what art historians call "The Iconography of Art" and it is the topic of this book. It can be a dry subject, and we have endeavored to lighten it up in places, restraining the impulse only in Chapter Five, in which the topic is no laughing matter. It has been a grand adventure over time to have had the opportunity to see so much of the artistic legacy bequeathed to us. Its vital importance is such that worldwide great buildings stand filled with treasures for all the world's people to admire. It has been such a satisfaction to research the subject of iconography, and even more pleasing to write about it. We hope you will enjoy it and enjoy the elucidating "tools" – images, tables, footnotes – that facilitate looking at art works in a more complete and edifying way. We don't pretend to have the final word on the subject, as, in words of Michelangelo: '*Ancora imparo*" (I am still learning), each day is truly a new learning experience, but setting down what we have learned so far has reinforced in us the wish to share this knowledge with you.

1

In museums, 90 percent of Western art from the 10th through the 15th century had Christian themes. Additionally, there is a large body of now fading, flaking religious paintings that adorn the walls of medieval churches from as early as the 5th - 6th century. Seldom, one encounters a rescued work that has been successfully transferred to a panel for display in a museum. By the 16th century that figure dipped to about 75 percent, even as additional Old Testament subject matter in paintings emerged alongside Christ-centered works that featured saints. Hagiography had surfaced as Church canon law encouraged art to incorporate saintly personages and their Christian conceits. By the 17th century, following the emergence of Renaissance thought, humanistic themes increased dramatically, but overall, religious subjects still accounted for some 50 percent of art works. The dominance of religious art further decreased as post-Reformation iconoclasm increased, and art became more decorous in purpose, with mythological, classical allegory, domestic social scenes, still-lifes, landscapes and portraiture captivated the interest of most artists and their public. Throughout the 18th and 19th centuries, a body of religious, social and portraiture art continued, but a pronounced shift towards experimentation in color and light appeared, so that, by the 20th century, a revolutionary shift in a more secular age was reflected most dramatically in painting and sculpture. Gone were representational art and its iconology in favor of bold expressions of color and abstract forms, a phenomenon brilliantly elucidated by Robert Hughes (1938-2012) in *The Shock of the New*.

Blessedly, we remain inheritors of the glorious history of human expression and will examine here all representational art and its iconology to the 19th century. We begin with early Christian art suffused in the philosophy of *memento mori* (remember death) that reflected the superstition, fear of internecine wars, of plague, epidemics of all kinds, starvation, and, more than anything else, the fear of inescapable death.

In art with Christian themes, the aim was often to allay many fears with uplifting pious works laden with religious symbols. To their contemporaries, the meaning of the iconography would have been familiar, obvious in fact, much as the cross that represents the crucifixion of Christ remains evident to the modern viewer. Most iconographic symbols, however, now appear arcane, unfathomable, begging for explication. That was true for us until our curiosity took us to authorities who documented long obscure visual references in art and explained their meanings, such as the reason Christ's genitalia was depicted in paintings, or the relevance of red coral sometimes seen in the hands of the infant Jesus – eye openers that enriched our aesthetic experience. So, to begin....

2

The first demand any work of art makes upon us is surrender. Look. Listen. Receive. Get yourself out of the way. (There is no good asking first whether the work before you deserves such a surrender, for until you have surrendered you cannot possibly find out).

C.S. Lewis (1898-1963): *An Experiment in Criticism.*

Chapter One: Good Heavens! Religious Iconography

Artists embedded iconographic symbols in every artistic medium: on canvases, murals, stone sculptures, paper, etc. They are on view everywhere in compositions – held in hands, on clothing, somewhere in the background. Giovanni Bellini's (1430-1516) *Sacra Conversazione* (Fig. 1), in the church of San Zaccaria, Venice, serves as a model reference. Painted in 1505, the depiction of a traditional Madonna and infant Jesus complements the classical marble altar piece in which it is set with its architectural framework and domed niche, on top of which rests a sculpted head of an approving God like figure. The iconic Mary and Jesus, are seated, glorified, not with halos or golden adornments, but by the majesty conveyed by the elevated throne they sit on, their dignity, and the gravitas of four colorfully robed saints posed in perfect balance on each side of them. Melodic strains we sense emanating from the angel's musical instrument enhance the solemnity of the painting. The vibrant red and blue* of Mary's clothes are conventional to her, and here serve a compositional purpose as well, as the rich blue mantle flows downward to end at the feet of the figure on the left. Color in the painting overall has compositional importance, as does the saintly presence, all of whom, in their carriage, direct the eye to the central figures.

Bellini had enormous influence on countless successors who adopted his compositional style of a Madonna and Child flanked by saints and angels painted in dazzling color. The conceit, known as *sacra conversazione,* heightened a sense of spirituality and solemnity, and enabled artists to introduce a donor (the money guy) into the picture. Such tableaux in this

*Mary's blue would become the subject of the profanity outburst "sacre bleu."

era aimed to humanize Mary and Jesus, and certainly in Renaissance art, the depiction of Jesus' genitalia was the quintessential humanizing technique. The hitherto modest portrayals of the semi-nude Jesus yielded to an art movement called *ostentatio genitalium*.[1] It was not intended as spicy or scandalous, but to accentuate Christ's human nature.[2] In this painting, his divinity is not in doubt, evidenced by the authoritative gesture of his right hand in the act of a blessing.* Despite the absence of halos, the attendants on the Madonna and Child are identifiable as saints because of the iconography that has been forever attributed to their persons: We know it is St. Peter because he holds the Keys to the Kingdom. Just behind him is a martyr, symbolized by the palm frond. The broken wheel on which she was tortured identifies her as St. Catherine. Across from her is another martyr holding a frond, St. Lucy. The oil lamp is symbolic and gives her away, for her name derives from *lux* meaning light. St. Lucy is also often depicted with her eyes on a plate, as her persecutors, in one version of her martyrdom, had blinded her. St. Jerome, one of four Doctors of the Church with attendant illustrious stature in Church history, was a priest, theologian and scholar who translated the bible from Hebrew and the gospels from Greek into Latin. Spurning apocryphal gospels, Jerome's Latin Vulgate became the official version of the bible of the Roman Catholic Church. In this painting he is anachronistically dressed as a cardinal† with a copy of his bible in his hands. The iconography associated with St. Jerome is extensive, and each gives biographical data – cardinal robes and, most often, a cardinal's hat that befits a high ranking ecclesiastic, the books of a scholar, a skull as a reminder of mortality, and a lion, a reference to a story that he befriended a lion after he plucked a thorn from its paw (an anecdote that dated, in fact, to ancient times.) When occasionally portrayed dressed in rags, it is meant to recall the four years St. Jerome lived as a hermit in the wilderness; a stone alludes to self-flagellation to quell sexual thoughts, and a quill and ink pay tribute to his scholarship. This exquisite masterpiece, teeming with exegetical energy and aesthetic beauty, has one small, significant feature of all of Bellini's works: to the right of the angel seated on the base of the throne is a small rectangular *trompe-l'oeil* fold-creased paper bearing the signature of the painter.

---

*Note the thumb, index and middle finger extended with 4th and 5th fingers folded. In Eastern orthodox iconography, the 2nd and 3rd fingers are extended while the thumb touches the 4th finger.

†The office of Cardinal did not evolve until the 8th century.

Fig. 1. Giovanni Bellini. *Sacra Conversazione.*

Madonna and Child with Sts. Nicholas Bari, Catherine of Alexandria and a donor by Gentile da Fabriano (1370-1427) (Fig. 2), follows the Byzantine iconographic tradition with its golden, halo like, demi-lune background and the almost black deep blue hooded cloak and red gown Mary wears. The child offers a blessing, and a host of fiery bird like angels perched in the two symmetrically placed trees sing and play instruments that contribute to the solemn deific scene.[3] The new Humanism that had been introduced into Italy, however, defines the piece, and is evident in the exposed genitalia of the Christ Child and the childlike reach of his arm upwards towards his mother's face that all but embraces her. The tilted, fixed gaze of Mary towards the viewer and the decorative ground, so reminiscent of the *mille fleur* of medieval tapestry, also relate to the innovative style of the day. Mary's simple throne, adorned with two lilies at the base, signify her purity. Two saints are in attendance. St. Nicholas of Bari, with a crosier in his grip, dressed in a Bishop's regalia, is recognizable because of the three gold balls in his right hand that signify his fame for providing gold as dowry to poor women. The palm frond of the martyr St. Catherine identifies her, as does the miniature wheel of torture she crushes with her foot. The homunculus kneeling at the foot of Mary is the donor who paid for the painting. Donors in paintings are tiny or large – dependent, one supposes, on the size of their egos or the amount paid to the artist.

Fig. 2. Gentile da Fabriano. *Madonna and Child, Sts. Nicholas and Catherine and donor.*

Hagiographical portraits typically included the symbols or conceits that are traditionally associated with the subjects by which they can be identified. In *Madonna and Child with Four Evangelists and Angels* (c. 1400), Andrea di Bartolo (1389-1428) (Fig. 3) gives a nod to Eastern iconographic depictions of the Madonna with his lavish use of gold leaf in his composition that includes the Four Evangelists (sporting golden nimbuses) who wrote the four gospels of the New Testament. The energy in the work is purely Western: the saints engage with each other, eliciting Jesus' fidgety interest. Jesus is modestly dressed and beguilingly holds a goldfinch, a symbol of the resurrection. Sitting on Mary's lap, he is flanked by beatific and adoring angels and the four Evangelists with their attributes (derived from Revelations 4:7) that disclose their identity. On the left is Mark, with the haloed winged lion at his feet. The wings evoke his intention to disseminate the gospel *urbis et orbis*. Next to him stands John with a snake which is sometimes depicted in a chalice. Legend has it John was

6

given a cup of poisoned wine. He blessed the wine and the venom wormed its way out of the cup in the form of a snake. Matthew, with a winged man at his feet, references his gospel of Christ's genealogy and therefore his humanity. The winged ox at Luke's feet signifies Christ's sacrificial ministry and death on the cross, the emphasis in Luke's gospel. The ox is the animal most traditionally used for sacrifices in antiquity, its blood a symbol of expiation. Writers of 'The Good News' of Christ, each of the evangelists hold books and quills. Winged living figures, symbols of the evangelists, were favorite figures used by early Christian artists, and employed at a very early date. They are taken from the vision of Ezekiel 1:10 and the *Revelations* of St. John.

Fig. 3. Andrea di Bartolo. *Madonna and Child with Four Evangelists and Angels.*

Hagiographic conceits were often the focal point of paintings, such as Lorenzo Lippi's (1606-1665) *St. Agatha* (Fig. 4). A martyr, St. Agatha

7

was imprisoned and tortured – her breasts were lopped off with shears. She died about 251 CE. Lorenzo Lippi depicted her, unscathed, with both of her attributes – her breasts on a plate and the not-so-surgical shears.

Fig.4. Lorenzo Lippi. *St. Agatha.* (c. 1620).

Fig. 5. *St. Lawrence.*   Fig. 6. Anon. *St. Dominic.*

A Limoges polychrome enamel plaque of the late 16th century (Fig. 5) shows St. Lawrence holding the palm frond of a martyr, with, judging by the expression on his face, a seemingly fond hand on a large gridiron. He was a church deacon who distributed the wealth of the church to the poor. Imprisoned by a peeved prefect who returned the church property to the sacristies, he arranged to have Lawrence grilled in 258 CE. The smiling image bolsters his reputation as a man of humor. As he was being roasted on the grill, Lawrence supposedly quipped that he was satisfactorily well done on one side and said, "Turn me over." Saint Dominic (Fig. 6) was a Castilian priest and founder of the Dominican Order. He is the patron saint of hopeful mothers and has two major conceits – the rosary because of his Marian devotion and a dog carrying a torch. It seems his barren mother made a pilgrimage to the Abbey at Silo where she dreamed that a dog leapt from her womb carrying a torch in its mouth. Shortly thereafter Dominic quickened in her womb.

St. Bartholomew was one of the twelve apostles of Christ. How he was martyred is debated. Some say he was beaten and drowned, others, that he was crucified upside down and still others contend he was flayed alive. The latter was the one Christian iconographers and artists favor. Being skinned alive makes for great copy and certainly inspires dramatic images. Generally, he is showcased with the flayed skin and the knife used to skin him alive. Michelangelo's (1475-1564) *Last Judgment* (Fig. 7) in the Sistine Chapel has a somewhat spare representation of martyrs with their conceits. We only include a detail of that incredible work that parenthetically shows, just below Christ, St. Lawrence and, more interestingly, St. Bartholomew holding a swatch of flayed skin. The countenance on it, scholars, purport, is that it is of Michelangelo himself. We sometimes wonder what Freud would have made of that! Is that, as is claimed, a self-portrait as Holofernes on the Sistine Chapel ceiling? It certainly looks like him.*

*

Fig 7. Michelangelo. *Last Judgment* (detail).

Fig. 8. Cornelis. *Mary Magdalene in a Landscape.*

10

Albert Cornelis's (c. 1475-1532) kneeling figure incorporates many of the attributes identified with Mary Magdalene, a renowned saint closely identified with Jesus (Fig. 8). The red himation like gown is either a reference to her love for Jesus or to a checkered past. The cross is a sign she was present at the crucifixion. The conceits most often associated with her are a skull (not shown here) and, especially, a jar of ointment. John's gospel (12.3) describes how she anointed Christ's feet with ointment at the last supper. The kneeling figure might be any faithful orant, but the little white jar in the lower left of the canvas undisputedly refers to Mary Magdalene.

The painting of St. Peter the martyr is a stunner. In fact, he looks quite stunned as well. A 13th century Dominican priest from Verona, he was assassinated – you guessed it – with a hatchet through the skull. He was fast tracked to sainthood in only 11 months – an ecclesiastical record.

Fig. 9. Lorenzo Lotto *Madonna with Peter Martyr*. (1503).

In addition to the martyred saint, Lorenzo Lotto (1480-1556) has filled the canvas with instructive iconography. The saint is wearing a white habit with a black hooded cape – the Dominican "uniform" – and holds his palm frond. As noted previously, Mary is depicted wearing her iconic red and blue. She reaches out to pat John the Baptist (with his staff and animal skin) on the head, with a firm grip around Jesus who sits on her lap. Jesus raises his hand in a blessing to his cousin, who later in Christ's ministry, served an important role. The infant Jesus usually has his right hand cramped into a blessing.

The saintly figure of St. Denis is but one of several statues found in the left portal of Notre Dame (Fig. 10). The first bishop of Paris in the third century Roman city, his Christianity did him in. Legendarily, once decapitated, St. Denis simply bent down to pick up his head and walked several kilometers before he fell down dead. In the Pantheon, on the left bank in Paris, there is an image of him chasing his head rolling away in a gust of wind!

Fig. 10. St. Denis. Left portal of Notre Dame.

Religious iconography is such a brainteaser, compiled of archaic references to long forgotten individuals and their stories. The first table in the appendix serves as a check list that decode the symbols, and, in our experience, works of art become more intelligible, meaningful, enjoyable and appreciated. (Just keep in mind the guy with the hatchet and the gal with the breasts on a plate!). A caveat: the list is not complete. Only the better known saints are listed since the church catalogue of saints is so gigantic the Library of Congress could practically devote an entire wing to it.

♣

The many iconographic elements associated with Christianity displayed in churches, whether Roman or Orthodox Catholic or Protestant, appear in paintings, murals, frescoes, sculpture, wall reliefs and inscriptions, tombs, *gisants*, memorials and plaques are usually visual. But there are powerful religious symbols imbued in letters, such as the ubiquitous cross marked with the Latin letters, INRI, *Iesus Nazarenus, Rex Iudaeorum* (Jesus of Nazareth, King of the Jews). Take away the cross, and the letters still invoke an image of the crucifixion for Christians, just as a skull is a reminder of death – the *memento mori* of old. The Greek AΩ (alpha and omega) acknowledges God as the "beginning and the end," the XP (chi and rho) are the first two Greek letters of ΧΡΙΣΤΟΣ, Christ in English. The monogram IHS is from the first three letters in Greek of the name Jesus – ΙΗΣΟΥΣ. DOM is an abbreviation for *Deo Optimo Maximo*, the motto of the Order of St. Benedict, "To God, who is the best and the greatest." AMDG, the Jesuit motto, stands for *Ad maiorem Dei gloriam* and translates as "For the greater glory of God." All of these elements were routinely understood for millennia, but, in a world with waning religious observance, and certainly for non-Christians, there is some explaining to do.

The belief that religious images of any kind represent a form of idolatry* has been an Islamic and Hebraic precept since their beginnings, and, for centuries, that was the case in the Byzantine Rite. In the Roman Catholic West, with the Protestant Reformation, many sects adopted that conviction and eschewed all human imagery in art. Spare and simple houses of worship became the rule for Puritans, Calvinists and Anabaptists. During England's civil wars (1642-1651) there was wholesale iconoclastic destruction of all facets and symbols associated with Roman Catholicism and high church Anglicanism: altars and rails, rood screens, stained glass, paintings, statues, reliefs – even organs. Most Protestants throughout Europe, however, welcomed the dove, pelican, fish, anchor and ship in Christian churches as poignant symbolic references to God and Church. The dove as a symbol of the Holy Spirit derives from Luke's gospel (3:22), "and the Holy Spirit descended on Him in a bodily form like a dove." An ancient legend of the mother pelican who vulned herself to feed her blood to her offspring resonated with early Christians, reminded of Christ's shedding of blood and sacrifice on the cross, and so the pelican in early Christianity became a symbol of Christ. The *ichthys,* the Greek word for fish became an acrostic for *Iesous Christos Theou Yios Soter* – Jesus Christ, Son of God, Savior.

---

*In 726 Pope Leo III (750-816) banned all images claiming they promoted idolatry, but in 843 the edict was rescinded with arguments that the images were venerated as devotional aids, not worshipped, and that they facilitated the religious education of an illiterate population. Similarly, Byzantine Emperor Theophilus (829-842) in 832 had proclaimed an edict prohibiting every image of worship.

The anchor refers to belief in Christ; it is rooted in *Hebrews* 6:19, "We have this hope as an anchor for the soul, firm and secure," The ship, most commonly found in Scandinavian churches, has many Christian references: the symbol derives from an ancient reference to Noah's ark and as a metaphor that compares the Church to a tempest tossed ship in a sea of nonbelievers and persecutors that safely reaches shore with its Christian cargo (Fig. 12). It alludes to Christ protecting Peter and his crew on a storm tossed ship. Derived from the Latin *navis*, or ship, the central front to back area in a church is called the "nave."

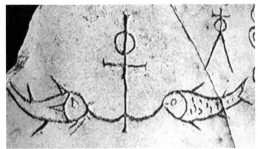

Fig. 11. Tomb slab from Catacomb of Domitilla, 3rd century CE with two Christian iconographs – anchor and fish.

Fig. 12. Ship model. Storkyrkan, Stockholm.

Iconographic symbols such as coral in the *Desco da parto* (Fig.13) by Bartolomeo di Fruosino (?1366-1441) for centuries were featured in works of art. Coral was believed to protect against seizures and evil spirits and was often worn as an amulet around children's necks, as in this painting, and used as an infant teething aid. Coral is often seen in the hands of the infant Jesus in paintings. A *Desco da parto,* traditionally twelve sided, a symbol of completeness, ritualistically and festively was presented to the mother after a successful delivery by her family and friends. They were popular mostly in Florence and Siena. Countless themes were painted on them, not just that of a child, and the *deschi* were meticulously decorated with painstaking, intricate detail. They still can be found in major galleries throughout the world.

Fig. 13. *Desco da parto.* Child with coral necklace and pinwheel.

The square nimbus was reserved for a holy person who was still living. The square nimbus surrounding the head of Pope John VII (Fig. 14), on a mosaic fragment in the Pinacoteca Vaticana, Rome, is a fine and early example (c.705).

Fig. 14. Square nimbus on Pope John VII (c.705).

♣

Secular iconography has roots in the Old Testament, in the moral philosophy of the ancients – Plato and Aristotle in Greece; Cicero and Marcus Aurelius in Rome – and form the core of the very Christian work, *Psychomachia* by Roman poet Aurelius. Several editions of this work, the first allegorical poem written, have illustrations of the Seven Virtues from which their symbols spring: Faith – a chalice or cross; Hope – an anchor. Charity had several emblems – a cornucopia, a heart, a nursing mother. Temperance had many signs as well, all associated with moderate behavior and restraint. It was most often represented by an exemplar pouring water from a jug into a vessel. Prudence was most often portrayed as a woman holding a mirror with a serpent. The mirror signified looking at the past and applying the wisdom attained from it to the present. The serpent represented knowledge. Courage or Fortitude was exemplified by a sword, and Justice by sword and a scale.

Seven Vices, known too as the Seven Deadly Sins, were often depicted, along with their particular infernal punishments: Lust is a cow punished by fire; Sloth, a goat or snail sentenced to a snake pit; Avarice or greed is a frog condemned to boil in oil; Wrath or Anger is a bear or lion slaughtered by dismemberment; Gluttony is a pig (what else?) damned to eat snakes and rats; Envy is a snake or dog condemned to immersion in freezing water for eternity (one would think this a more appropriate penance for

16

uncontrolled anger). Pride, considered the capital vice, was represented by a horse or peacock and the punishment was the dreaded wheel. First the bones were broken to facilitate weaving the extremities into the spokes of a wheel, and the offender was left to die.

All of the Seven Virtues and vices most famously appear in the frescoes by Giotto di Bondone (1266-1137) in the Scrovegni Chapel in Padua, three examples of which are shown here (Fig. 15).[4] Florentine Francesco Pesellino's (1422-1457) depicts *The Seven Virtues* (Fig.16) as beautiful female personifications, each with their symbolic attributes. The small male exemplars at their feet, five of whom hold the books of scholars, are theologians and authors. There appears to be a saint or two amongst them, virtuous men all.

Fig. 15. Giotto. *Justice, Envy, Charity.* Scrovegni Chapel, Padua (1300-1305).

Ambrogio Lorenzetti's (1290-1348) frescoes of *Good Government* and *Bad Government* are in the City Hall of Siena. The allegories have a superfluity of iconography – too far-reaching to fully elucidate here. *Good Government* (Fig. 17) portrays the Commune of Siena personified as a crowned king, seated on a throne with Wisdom hovering above him. Around his head are the letters C S C V – *commune saenorum civitatis virginis*. He is flanked by virtues. *Bad Government* (Fig. 18), on the other hand, has as its central figure a fanged Tyrammides (tyranny). Below him, Justice is bound in a death shroud flanked by figures of evil, as Avarice and Pride hover above her.

17

Fig. 16. Pesellino. *The Seven Virtues.* Florence (c. 1450)

18

Fig. 17. Lorenzetti. *Allegory of Good Government.* Siena (1338).

Fig. 18. Lorenzetti. *Allegory of Bad Government.* Siena (1338).

The example of virtues and vices by Hieronymus Bosch (c. 1450-1516) (Fig. 19), now in the Prado, is an extraordinary work rich in iconography and thematic process. The small circles, beginning in the top left, portray Death, then Judgment (top right), followed by Salvation (bottom right) and Condemnation on the left. The large circle characterizes the Seven Deadly Sins, beginning with Wrath or Anger on the bottom and, proceeding clockwise, Envy, Greed, Gluttony, Sloth, Lust and Pride. The Velasquez Gallery is a must when visiting the Prado, but skipping the Bosch painting would miss the boat of seeing a great work of art.

Fig. 19. Bosch. *Seven Deadly Sins and the Four Last Things* (c. 1500)

Dutchman Hieronymus Bosch (c. 1450-1516) left no letters, diaries or records. Nothing is known about his life and he left no guides for the interpretation of his fantastic narratives and iconography.[5] We can, however, from careful analysis of his work deduce that he had an uncanny understanding of human foibles, desires and fears and that he influenced a number of painters – most prominently Pieter Brueghel the Elder.

Footnotes: Chapter One

1. Steinberg, Leo. *The Sexuality of Christ in Renaissance Art and in Modern Oblivion.* New York: Pantheon, 1983.

2. The humanity of Jesus was revealed by exhibiting his genitalia as well as by depictions of childhood gestures and mischief. Images of *Maria gravitas* (pregnant) and *Maria lactans* (nursing) also served to inform the topos of the humanity of Jesus. A Gnostic manuscript, the *Evangelium Infantiae,* better known as the "Arabic Gospel of the Infancy" relates apocryphal stories from the "secret" life of Jesus that also humanize the son of God. There are extant Arabic and Syriac copies in the Vatican and the Bibliothèque Nationale. This gospel relates many mischievous activities of the toddler and latent child Jesus, which furthers the Nestorian concept of the human Jesus. Images inspired by this gospel were often depicted during the early Renaissance. Examples are a series of tiles from the fourteenth century Tring Parish church (outside of London), now in the British Museum, that portray Jesus in school and, common to pupils, show him being disciplined. A woodcut from a 1476 German book shows Jesus being taken to school by his mother (Deutches Buch Museum). Almost all artists of the period grappled to depict a very human Jesus.

One curiosity of Renaissance naturalism is that artists commonly disregarded Christ's circumcision that was cited in the New Testament. Perhaps it was, as Steinberg contended, that Christian artists "resisted the mark of it as an imperfection," or it was considered unaesthetic. It may be the artistic community sought to conceal Christianity's origins, which, in the words of Thomas Cahill in *Mysteries of the Middle Ages* began as "a miniscule sect of Judaism," and their art avoided intimations of Christ's Jewish heritage. For whatever reasons, these painters failed in exegetic accuracy, and depictions of a circumcised Jesus are rare. The authors are aware of only four, by Michelangelo, Biagio d'Antonio, David and Rubens, all of whom sculpted or painted a circumcised babe.

3. These might be Seraphim despite the absence of the requisite number of wings, but they are fiery red. Early medieval Christian theologians created a pecking order hierarchy of angels with nine celestial orders: Seraphim, Cherubim, Thrones, Dominions, Virtues, Powers, Principalities, Archangels and Angels, as described by Pseudo Dionysius (c. 5th century) in *De Coelesti Hierarchia.* Seraphim continuously praise God and are depicted as fiery six-winged creatures. (It is unclear how many could be placed on the head of a pin).

4. In Giotto's figure of *Justice*, if orthogonal lines are drawn from the front of the throne, the convergence will fall somewhere behind the figure in traditional internal perspective. We raise this obvious point because in *reverse perspective*, the convergence is between the image and the viewer – and this in itself can be an iconographic element since it appears almost exclusively in Byzantine icons of the 10th through 13th centuries, as seen in the example *The Annunciation*. It is an anonymous work from the Church of Climent in Ohrid, Macedonia circa 1300. On occasions, Cubists also used reverse perspective.

5. Care is required in the study of iconography, because meanings sometimes changed over centuries. The Patristic rose – symbolic of secrecy – for example became the Renaissance rose of Christ. In Egyptian hieroglyphics the child was depicted with a finger in the mouth. Harpocrates, the child manifestation of Horus, was portrayed in this manner and was interpreted by the Greek to represent "silence." Mythology reveals that Aphrodite presented Eros with a rose which he, in turn, gave to Harpocrates, asking him to keep secret the indiscretions of Aphrodite. Thus the rose became

the symbol of secrecy, and appeared on confessionals, council chambers, and on ceilings as rosettes. *Sub rosa* entered the lexicon to refer to any confidential, off the record secret verbal exchange. *En passant*, ancient Egyptian culture had a remarkably rich iconographic tradition of which finger-to-mouth Harpocrates is but one of thousands. Other examples include the ankt (symbol of life), Anubis the jackal-headed god – a psychopomp who weighed the hearts of the dead – the scarab symbolic of new life, the eye of Horus, the *wedjat* protector of health, etc. Well, anymore and it would necessitate a new book. Besides, it would violate this theme of Western iconography.

Parenthetically, some icons were evanescent; that is to say, symbols such as the *transi*, the measuring staff of the gravedigger, were in vogue only from the 14th through the 16th centuries – a relatively brief period of time – and they pertained only to adults and apocalyptic art (See Chapter Five).

Everything that man esteems
Endures a moment or a day.
Love's pleasure drives his love away,
The painter's brush consumes his dreams.

William Butler Yeats (1865-1939) in The Tower

Chapter Two: Ye gods! Iconography of Mythology and Allegory

OLYMPIAN MYTHOLOGY

Fast on the heels of late medieval art, came the great Arabic translational movement[1] and the Renaissance, in which Greek gods and their Roman derivatives, lost during the rise of Christianity and barbarian incursions, reappeared, resurrected in mythology and allegory, many names quickly remembered because they were written in the stars as constellations and in the zodiac. The classics of antiquity, returned to Europe by the Arabs (some scholars, like Thomas Cahill, also include Irish and English monks[2]), gave rise to new humanistic themes and initiated a slow but progressive decline in the output of religious art. The secular found expression. Thematic allegory such as Lorenzetti's *Good and Bad Government* led the way, but with the "rediscovery" of the classics, the depiction of mythology emerged as favorite subjects. Artists justified this "pagan" art in a world still dominated by the Roman Catholic Church by highlighting whatever morality they could find ingrained in mythological tales and heroes.

Admittedly, much of mythological art was painted *ars gratia artis* or for the challenge of depiction, but at the beginning of the artistic movement of mythological themes, many were painted with moral purpose. Michelangelo Buonarroti (1475-1564) comes to mind, with his inclusion in the Sistine Chapel's *Last Judgment,* of Charon, who, in the ancient world was the boatman who rowed souls to Hades, where Minos, who became the judge of the dead (Fig. 20), greeted them.

24

Fig. 20. Michelangelo's *Last Judgment* (detail). Note Charon swinging an oar, and, Minos with snake.[3]

Peter Paul Rubens's (1577-1640) *Allegory of the Blessings of Peace* (Fig. 21), a stark contrast between Peace and War, could not be more revealing. He was an emissary who hoped to parlay a peace between warring England and Spain. In the painting, Minerva (Greek: Athena), goddess of wisdom, personified here as *Pax,* forces Mars (Greek: Ares), the god of war, and one of the Furies, Alecto in both Greek and Roman mythology, from the idyllic pastoral scene. To the left of the canvas, nymphs arrive, one bringing treasures and the other music. Ceres, the goddess of earth, her back to Mars and the Fury as they flee, dispenses a stream of the breast milk of charity* to a toddler and surveys with satisfaction the abundance that surrounds her. A winged *putto* above Ceres's head extends an olive wreath and the caduceus of Mercury, symbols of peace. A leopard and satyr, symbols of the popular Bacchus, the god of fertility and wine (Greek: Dionysus) pull on a chariot full of fruit. Hymen, god of marriage, leads children to the cornucopia, as a *putto* and a torch bearer welcome them. It is not lost on the toddler – or the viewer – that Ceres has an impressive letdown reflex. In another opus, Rubens portrays Hera's breast milk creating the Milky Way in a dazzling display.

Mythology in the hands of the humanist served to teach life lessons, to illustrate virtues, to teach civility and establish a code of comportment. Unlike Christian themes, mythology was not concerned with redemption or salvation. Mythology conferred meaning and consequence to earthly behavior. It also provided inspiration to glorify the human body now possible as the growing cadre of anatomists *cum* artists such as da Vinci,

*A theme within a theme. Breast feeding is an emblem of *Caritas.*

25

Fig. 21. Rubens' *Allegory of the Blessings of Peace* (1629).

Michelangelo, Dürer, della Pietro, Kalcar, and d'Arate refined their skills, achieving the grace and beauty seen in ancient Greek works by Phidias (c. 480-430 BCE), Praxiteles (c. 400-330 BCE) and Lysippos (fl. 4th cent BCE). This is not to say that the religious iconography of *memento mori, vanitas* and the *transi* disappeared (more on them in another chapter), but a passion emerged to accurately depict the human body, and in doing so, artists forever changed Western art. With a single painting, Sandro Botticelli (1445-1510) ushered in an entirely new and original artistic vision. It was the first, and largest (six feet by nine feet), canvas painted in the Renaissance, with a mythological theme and a departure from the, until then, favored medium of painting on wood. Botticelli's ethereal masterpiece *The Birth of Venus* (Fig. 22) (Greek: Aphrodite), astonished his contemporaries with its beauty and daring. Despite the innocent purity of the nude Venus evident in the gestures of modesty and in her expression, it would have scandalized the demagogue Savanarola.[4]

The graceful and beautifully balanced composition with pleasing allegorical figures on each side of the breathtakingly beautiful Venus shows her, having risen from the sea, poised, in classic *contrapposto*, on a scallop shell* Modestly, her hand guides trusses of her hair to hide her pudenda.

*Parenthetically, Venus was born from sea foam, which was said to be rich in protein because the castrated testicles of Uranus had been thrown into the sea by Cronos at the command of Gaia.

On the left, the wind god Zephyr (Roman: Favonius), tightly holds the abducted (later his wife) Chloris (Roman: Flora), a nymph of spring whose signature flowers are sprinkled about. Zephyr blows a robust breeze that whips Venus's hair and the elegant robe for Venus one of the Horae, (goddesses of the seasons) holds in her hands as she floats forward towards the goddess of love.

Fig. 22. Botticelli. *Birth of Venus* (1482).

Donato di Niccolò di Betto Bardi (Donatello) (1386-1466) and after him Michelangelo were Renaissance artists who glorified the human body in their works, but Botticelli's Venus (although anatomically quirky) was stunning and lithe compared, say, to the anatomically accurate but massive and lithic torsos of Michelangelo. In 1514, writing of Michelangelo, da Vinci said, "O anatomical painter. Beware, lest in the attempt to make your nudes display all their emotion by a too strong indication of bones, sinews and muscles, you become a wooden painter."[5]

Mythological topics proliferated in art works thereafter that exhibited energy and fervor, anatomical accuracy and had a complex focus on narrative. Zeus (Roman: Jupiter) was the most often featured mythological persona whom Ovid, in *Metamorphoses,* described as an oversexed rake intent on seducing every pretty little thing he saw, employing deception whenever expedient to his nefarious intentions. We elected to compile a Table (that extends to three pages!) in the appendix to illustrate the point. Yes. There were that many conquests. He was, after all, king of the gods, and, in the words of Mel Brooks, "It's good to be the king." There are, however, other arresting figures from the mythological realm immortalized in art who are noteworthy.*

♣

Europa. Lovely thing. Daughter of a Phoenician king, and Zeus lusted after her. True to his *modus operandi* of inventive subterfuge, he transformed himself into a gentle looking white bull. He wandered into the king's herd and there was Europa in the field gathering flowers when she was attracted to this remarkable *bos taurus*. She approached him, rubbed his back and impulsively hopped onto his posterior. (What was she thinking?) Well, Zeus surely said to himself, "gotcha" and galloped off with her, headed to the sea. He swam to Crete where he revealed himself and ravished the girl. A son, Minos, was the result. Tiziano Vecellio, better known as Titian (c. 1498-1576) portrayed a spicy version of the episode (1562) – complete with Eros/Cupid and associates aiding and abetting the seduction (Fig. 23).

Fig. 23. Titian. *The Abduction of Europa.*

*One caveat. Greek mythology comes in many flavors because there were many cooks. There's the *Metamorphosis* of Ovid, the *Theogony* of Hesiod, Homer's *Odyssey* and *Iliad*, the anonymous *Homeric Hymns* and others. We have elected to describe the most common and popular versions of the myths and to match them up with their respective depictions.

Leda. With this delectable dish, Zeus assumed the guise of a swan and seduced Leda while she selflessly embraced and shielded him from an attacking eagle. (Zeus had this thing about eagles – reference Prometheus, Ganymede and Aigina). She subsequently laid two eggs (double yolkers), one of which resulted in Helen of Troy and Pollux, and the other, Castor and Clytemnestra. This was a very popular seduction that artists liked to paint, soft and downy, if you'll excuse the expression, and frequently depicted in painting and sculpture. The painting by Cesare da Sesto (1477-1523) is a copy (1515) of the original by da Vinci, now lost (Fig. 24). The extraordinary graphic sculpture is a Roman copy of an Attic original 1st century BCE (Fig 25).

There is another version of this myth which relates that the first egg was fertilized by *Zeus*, but the second by Leda's legit husband, Tyndareus, King of Sparta. Thus, *Castor* and *Pollux* were fraternal twins together called the *Dioscuri* – the *Gemini*. They are considered the patrons of sailors and manifest themselves as St. Elmo's fire (a plasmic coronal discharge from a pointed object in an electron charged field such as a thunderstorm) – didn't expect science stuff here – did you?

Fig. 24. Sesto (after da Vinci) *Leda and the Swan.*   Fig. 25. Roman copy of Attic *Leda and the Swan.*

Danaë. The only child of the king of Argos – another stunner on whom Zeus had his wily eye. He presented himself to her as a shower of gold and impregnated her. Voila! – Perseus. No wait, it's not over. The king, having been told by an oracle that Perseus would kill him, cast both mother Danaë and infant into the sea locked in a chest. This piqued Zeus's rage, and he commanded Poseidon to calm the sea and rescue the pair. The chest washed ashore on the island of Seriphos (map on page 42), where Dictys found mother and infant, protected her and raised the child. In 1908 Léon Francois Comerre (1850-1916) painted Danaë enveloped in ecstasy (Fig. 26).

Como pasan los años …. Perseus, grown to be a handsome muscular specimen, was commanded to get the head of Medusa. He was given a little help with Athena's shield, Hermes's winged sandals and Hades's helmet of invisibility. He stalked Medusa, protecting himself from a fatal direct gaze by looking at her only in the reflection of his shield, thereby averting a lithic marbling as he proceeded to decapitate the serpentine coiffed wench. WOW! What a story! Out of a shower of gold came Zeus who produced Perseus who slay the invincible, indomitable, ugly Medusa. Benvenuto Cellini (1500-1571) crafted Perseus in 1545. It is in Florence in the Loggia dei Lanzi (Fig. 27).

Fig. 26. Comerre. *Danaë.*

30

Fig. 27. Cellini. *Perseus and Head of Medusa.*

Io. In his seduction of Io, the princess of Argos, Zeus covered the world with a thick cloud as a cloaking device to hide her from his wife, Hera. But wise to his tricks, she descended from Mount Olympus to disperse the cloud. Zeus quickly disguised Io by turning her into a white heifer. Hera sensed the ruse, so she asked for the cow as a gift. How could Zeus refuse? Hera sent the cow into pasture and asked the hundred-eyed Argus Panoptes to guard it. Zeus impulsively sent Hermes to fetch Io and, disguised as a shepherd, Hermes sang and lulled Argus into sleep and killed him. As a tribute to Argus, Hera took his 100 eyes and set them into the tail of her favorite bird, the peacock, and sent the biggest of all gadflies to bite the bovine, Io, who escaped, but wandered the world in a state of madness until she eventually recovered her human form. Sir Walter Scott's "What a tangled web we weave when first we practice to deceive" was simplistic when compared to Greek and Roman mythology! It suffices to simply appreciate the whopping paw of a cloud that engulfs Io in this work by Antonio Allegri da Correggio (1489-1534), painted in 1530 (Fig. 28). Take note of the expression of rapture similar to that of the enchanted Danaë.

31

Fig. 28. Correggio. *Jupiter and Io* (1530).

Greek mythology was cosmological. It aimed to reveal the origins of the universe through an oral tradition of narrative poetics, which in turn gave rise to the visual narratives of vase depiction, *exvotos* and sculptures. The oldest sources are probably Homer's *Iliad* and *Odyssey* (c. 750 BCE) which relate stories of a Bronze Age conflict – the Trojan war (c. 1200 BCE) – between Troy and Mycenaean Greece. Archeological discoveries of 8th century geometric pottery with references to the epic tale helped preserve the mythology in people's minds.

Allegorical representations of the gods on ceilings, in murals, tapestries, mosaics, Greek vases and reliefs as well as in sculptures and paintings always are identifiable by the symbols incorporated into the work. As with representations of saints, the gods had personalized conceits, and sometimes more than one. A common link between saints and roguish gods – who would have thought it? Table 4 lists the gods, with both their Greek and Roman names and insignia. Four examples follow: Athena with her owl, spear and helmet (Fig. 29) is depicted on a Greek red attic plate by Oltos (c. 520 BCE). Poseidon holds his trident in a 2nd century CE Roman mosaic in Palermo (Fig.30). The painting by Alexandre Cabanel (1823-1889) is of Swedish soprano Christine Nilsson (1843-1921) in the guise of Pandora holding her evil filled box (Fig. 31). The final example is a Roman bronze after the Greek Lysippos of a resting Hermes with his winged sandals (Fig.32).

Fig. 29. Athena with her owl. Red-Attic plate.

Fig. 30. Mosaic of Poseidon. Palermo.

Fig. 31. Cabanel. *Pandora.*

34

Fig. 32. *Hermes* (after Lysippos), Naples.

There are, to be sure, universal legendary themes that give rise to comparative mythology. The Great Flood is perhaps the best example, for every culture with literary and oral traditions has just such a story, most notable in Genesis and in the great Mesopotamian work of Gilgamesh. Greek mythology's Deucalion, son of Prometheus, confronted a flood created by Zeus and, like Noah, built a vessel and thereby escaped with his wife Pyrrha. Common topics are Paradise Lost and the Apocalypse, often referred to as the Triumph of Death. Battles of the gods such as the Greek Olympians vs the Titans and the Hindu Devas vs Asuras were trendy. The Heroic Quest is a universal literary theme, as in the *Iliad* and *Odyssey, The Aeneid, Gilgamesh, Sinbad and 1001 nights,* the Arthurian legends and others, that have also been depicted in art, many famously depicted in collosal sizes.

That is particularly so of depictions of the great biblical flood. Antonio Carracci's (1583-1618) painting (Fig. 33) measures 166 by 247 cm. or almost 5 and ½ by 8 feet. Gilgamesh, king of Assyria and the lion (Fig. 34), dressed in royal Assyrian garments, stands imperially 5 meters tall in the Louvre in Paris. In contrast, *The Battle of the Gods* (Fig. 35) by Cesare Rossetti (c.1565-1623), a meager 66 by 88 cm (~ 2.2 by 2.9 feet) proves art should not be measured not by its size, but by its quality.

Fig. 33. Carracci. *The Flood* (c. 1617)

Fig. 34. *Gilgamesh.*

Fig. 35. Rossetti. *Battle of the Gods.*

Zeus grew up hiding from his filicidal cannibalistic father, and one day he slipped him an emetic potion that caused *Cronus* to vomit up all of *Rhea's* children – undigested, fully assembled and grown. *Zeus* and his siblings challenged *Cronus*, defeated the entire Titan clan and were forever after referred to as the Olympians. With the defeat of the Titans, the Olympians, under the thumb of *Zeus*, lived on Mount Olympus where he controlled both gods and mortals. There was a bevy of unforgettable *dramatis personae*: *Nymphs, Naiads, Dryads, Nereids, Satyrs,* and others. Their shenanigans lend themselves to irreverent iconographic examination (if it's not too much a bother).

♣

Although there are many Roman representations derived from Greek mythology – some of which are exact copies and a small number unique to Rome – virtually all mythology depicted allegorically in the western world is Greek, but often referred to with their Roman appellations. Here presented are 40 plus myths that constitute the Greek canon most frequently recreated over the centuries in painting, sculpture, mosaic, pottery, tapestry and other media. Almost certainly, 90 percent of mythological *cum* allegorical art scattered throughout the museums of the world refers to one of these forty. Familiarity with their themes, therefore, confers an almost comprehensive understanding of all of the extant highly charged artistic soap operas for one's globe hopping museum pleasure, and, standing before an opus and intoning to absolutely no one in particular, one might be inclined to mutter, "Ah, yes …of course."

The Trojan war was instigated when the married Helen of Sparta took off with Trojan prince Paris. Her husband, Menelaus and the Mycenaean king Agamemnon set out to reclaim her. The warriors engaged in the subsequent hostilities were a pantheon of Greek heroes such as Achilles and Odysseus who crossed the Aegean and laid siege to Troy. The war lasted ten years until the Greek army departed, leaving behind the gift of a large wooden horse which Laocoön rightly feared would win, place or show for the Greek State, not Troy.

Odysseus. Famously depicted on a myriad of Greek vases and in paintings, the king of Ithaca is the stuff of legendary heroes. As he yearned and strove to return home to his beloved family, he confronted adversity and misadventure on a monumentally heroic scale. Odysseus was the model figure of dogged persistence, stamina and faithfulness who embodied the greatest virtues of the Greeks. His trials and tribulations spawned great visual copy derived from Homer's mighty epic poem *The Odyssey*. The painting by Draper Herbert James (1863-1920) in the Ferens Gallery, Kingston upon Hull, England (Fig. 36), depicts the episode from *The Odyssey* in which Odysseus faces mortal danger from Sirens, whose enchanting and bewitching music was said to lure men in ships to their deaths upon the shore's rocks. As in Homer's tale, forewarned by Circe, Odysseus is seen bound by his men to the mast of his ship, ears plugged with beeswax, as they anxiously row past the Island of the Sirens. Three Sirens, two of whom have shed their mermaid scales upon boarding the ship, are shown vainly enticing a terrified Odysseus to his doom. Draper transformed the ugly, hideous creatures of Greek imagination into sensuous, seductive beauties, lending visual credence to the irresistibility of their annihilative siren song. An iconic depiction of the saga is the Attic red stamnos vase c. 480 BCE (Fig. 37) on which Sirens (Harpies) fancifully appear as birds with women's heads hovering over the ship that carries the restrained Odysseus safely past the Island of the Sirens.

Fig. 36. James. *Odysseus and the Sirens.*

38

Fig. 37. Attic vase of *Odysseus and the Harpies.*

Jason and the Argonauts. This is a complex myth that can easily be simplified as essentially Jason's quest to prove worthy of his kingdom, and he does so by setting sail on the Argo to claim the golden fleece. Among his crew of heroes are Boreads, Hercules, Philoctetes, Peleus, Telamon, Orpheus, Castor, Pollux, Atalanta, Meleager and Euphemus. Their journey is marred by misadventure, deception, tectonic crushing rocks, carrion harpies with dragon teeth and the bronze giant Talos. It is a story of superheroes if ever there was one, and thousands of art works and literary renditions attest to its popularity. Here, *Jason with the Golden Fleece* is by Erasmus Quellinus II (1607-1678) (Fig. 38).

Fig. 38. Erasmus Quellinus II. *Jason with the Golden Fleece.*

Orpheus and Eurydice. Orpheus, son of the muse Calliope and Apollo, played a lyre that transfixed all living creatures. He married the beautiful Eurydice, and they were ecstatically happy until the shepherd Aristaeus saw Eurydice in a forest one day. Instantly enamored, he chased after her, and, as she fled, she was bitten by a snake and died. Orpheus' grief was profound, but Apollo told him to stop his blubbering and go to hell and, as a dutiful son, he did. Descending into Hades to fetch Eurydice, he encountered and vanquished the three headed Cerberus before advancing to an audience with Hades and Persephone, king and queen of the underworld. He played his lyre for them and, enchanted, they released Eurydice to him on condition that he not look at her during their ascent out of Hades. Well, you know what happened, right? He looked at her and, poof, she was gone! This compelling, tragically romantic story has been the stuff of opera and ballet. There is even a movie of the story, set in the favelas of Brazil in 1959, called *Black Orpheus*. Great flick. The painting of the calamity, finished in 1878, is by John Stanhope (1829-1908) (Fig. 39). The artist inventively included another famous myth into the painting – Charon the psychopomp, who carried souls on the river Styx to Hades.

Fig. 39. Stanhope. *Orpheus and Eurydice on the banks of the Styx.*

Daedalus and Icarus. This allegorical morality tale of hubris was and is renowned. The protagonists wished to escape from Crete, and Daedalus fabricated wings for Icarus and himself, attaching them with wax. Daedalus

40

warned his son not to get too close to the heat of the sun, lest the wax melt and the wings fall off. They flew off and over the Aegean Sea, passing Delos and Samos, when Icarus, having forgotten his father's admonition, cockily flew towards the sun. Drip. The wax melted and Icarus fell to his death. Ah, but mythology to the rescue! All was not lost. Icarus was transformed into the island of Icaria (Ikarie). (Map on page 42). In the painting by Anthony van Dyke (1599-1641) (Fig. 40), Daedalus issues a somber warning, finger pointing ominously upwards to the sun. But since when does a kid listen to his father?

Fig. 40. Van Dyke. *Daedalus and Icarus*

The Aegean Sea has over 2,000 islands, the largest among them is Crete (Kriti). Settled by the ancient Greeks, the sea features prominently in many Greek myths. In addition to Icarus and Daedalus, Theseus and the Minotaur, Jason and the Argonauts and Odysseus, there are more myths associated with the Cyclades, some of which are mentioned here. When the ship of King Koiranos of Syros sank, a dolphin rescued him and carried him to a cave; in Tinos, Hercules killed the sons of Vorias – the god of the north winds; on his way to recover the Golden Fleece; Jason landed on the island of Anaphe, where Euphemus, son of Poseidon, threw a clod of the Anaphean earth into the sea and the volcanic island of Thera appeared (Thera blew up c. 1600 BCE and destroyed Crete's capitol, Knossos. Later, Thera's name was changed to Santorini); in Naxos, Ariadne was abandoned by Theseus, where Dionysus found her and married her.

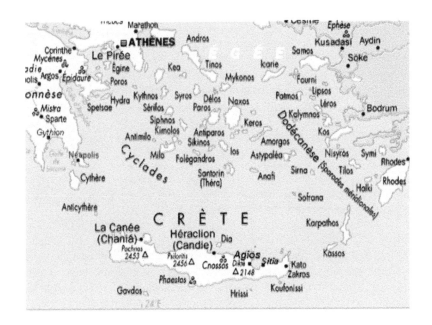

Fig. 41. The *Wounded Amazon*.

Amazonai. These were tribes of warrior women who lived in isolated areas. They had no time for men except for procreation purposes to sustain their numbers. Otherwise their encounters were combative confrontations. The Amazonai raised female offspring and sent male newborns to their fathers. It is said they amputated their right breasts to facilitate drawing arrows from their quivers, and their name may derive from *a mostos* – without breast. None of the depictions we have encountered, however, substantiate the claim. In mythology, Queen Penthesilea fought in the Trojan War, and her sister Hippolyta had her girdle stolen by Herakles. The *Wounded Amazon* (Fig. 41) is from an original by Phidias (c. 480-430 BCE).

Theseus. King of Athens was, of all things, married to an Amazon. That's mythology for you! He had superhero powers, and rid Athens of the Minotaur, a half-man, half-bull monster who demanded the sacrifice of children and animals. The Minotaur lived in a labyrinth made by Daedalus. Theseus stealthily entered it. Tying a ball of string at the entrance, he found the Minotaur, killed it and followed the string that guided him out of the labyrinth. *Theseus and the Minotaur* (Fig. 42), sculpted in 1782 by Antonio Canova (1757-1822), is now in the Victoria and Albert Museum in London.

Fig. 42. Canova. *Theseus and the Minotaur.*

43

Perseus and Andromeda. Remember Perseus and the slain Medusa? He's a superhero twice over, and this tale tells how and why. Andromeda was the daughter of Cepheus and Cassiopeia, who boasted of their daughter's beauty, saying it surpassed the beauty of the sea nymphs, the Nereids. The Sea God Poseidon was infuriated by this boast and sent Cetus the sea monster to devour Andromeda. Stripped of her clothing and chained to a rock awaiting her fate, she was found by Perseus, who had been returning home in triumph after doing away with Medusa. He angrily killed Cetus, released Andromeda, married her, and the two lived happily ever after, as they say. Did we mention he travelled around in the air, thanks to a borrowed winged helmet and sandals that made him invisible and which he never returned? In the lavish painting of the myth that hangs in the Hermitage in St. Petersburg, Charles-André van Loo (1705-1765) (Fig. 43), Perseus, helmet and sandals in full view, dives towards the monster.

Fig. 43. van Loo. *Perseus and Andromeda.*

Pygmalion and Galatea. This allegory of Pygmalion's obsessive love for the beautiful marbleized Galatea (Greek for white stone) he sculpted was first recounted by Ovid in *Metamorphosis*. The statue, in Pygmalion's view, embodied the purity and virtue he thought was lacking in all women. In Galatea, the lonely artist's yearning for love had hope of fulfillment. Call it

44

virtual reality. As the story goes, he couldn't keep his hands off her, kissed her, dressed her and longed for her to become a living, breathing creature. After making a supplicating offer to Venus to breathe life into Galatea, he returned to his studio, dashed to the object of his desire and kissed the statue. *Voila!* There are many depictions of this myth, but the Met in New York claims this wowser, painted by Jean-Leon Gerome (1824-1904) in 1890 (Fig. 44). It shows the moment when the iconographic Cupid propels its arrow of love and Galatea is transformed into a living soul mate to Pygmalion. Towering over Pygmalion as she does, it poses the question, who's in charge here? Our bet is on Galatea. Gerome has packed the painting with iconographic images: a woman with a child, suggesting the purpose of a romantic union, awe struck Greek theatrical masks that emphasize the fantasy of it all and even a vanity conceit of a woman who admires herself in a mirror.

Fig. 44. Gerome. *Pygmalion and Galatea.*

Fig. 45. Bernini. *The Abduction of Proserpine.*

Persephone. (Roman: Proserpine). The daughter of Zeus and Demeter, Persephone was abducted by Hades, who named her Queen of the Underworld. Without her, earth became barren, and people starved. Zeus forced Hades to allow Persephone to return to the world, and Hades agreed, but cagily gave her a pomegranate to eat, the consequence of which destined her to return to the underworld during the winter months. In the spring, summer and fall, however, the earth, through her good graces, was fertile again, ensuring an abundance of food. The allegory of the seasons is embedded in this myth. Gian Lorenzo Bernini (1598-1680) sculpted the electrifying *Abduction of Proserpine* (Fig. 45) in 1622 with mind-blowing artistry and plasticity in which the marble cedes to his skill. Note the indentations Hades' fingers imprint on her thighs. The Villa Borghese in Rome is the museum lucky enough to have this masterpiece.

46

Prometheus. He was the benefactor of mankind who brought fire from Mount Olympus to mortals on earth. As punishment, Zeus chained him to a rock and ordered an eagle to eat his naturally regenerating liver daily* There are many paintings of this myth, but the most spectacular is the collaborative work of Peter Paul Rubens (1577-1640) and Frans Snyders (1579-1657) (Fig. 46).

Fig. 46. Rubens and Snyders. *Prometheus.*

*Zeus, in another allegorical tale, seduced Elara, who then was with child. Zeus concealed her from his wife, Hera, by burying her beneath the earth. The embryo grew so humongous, Elara's womb split open. The goddess of earth, Gaia, went to the rescue and carried the fetus to term. A boy, he was named Tityos. Well, the apple doesn't fall far from the tree. When Tityos matured, he attempted to seduce Leto, one of Zeus's conquests. Zeus punished him by having his body tied down and stretched out on a large rock in the abyss of Tartarus. There, for eternity, two vultures dined on his liver daily. Michelangelo magnificently sketched the myth as only he could do as a love note to his beloved Tommaso de Cavalieri. In the Prado is a harrowing – and phenomenal – version of the story by Jusepe de Ribera (1591-1652).

47

Fig. 47. Poussin. *Midas and Bacchus.*

King Midas. The fable is a legend about avarice and greed and their consequences. A drunk Silenus, found by peasants, was delivered to King Midas of Phrygia, who recognized him as a friend of the Roman god of wine, Bacchus. Midas extended generous hospitality to the satyr before returning him to his master, and Bacchus expressed his appreciation by granting the king one wish. Midas asked that everything he touched turn to gold. Disastrous mistake. Sure, a branch and a stone he touched turned to gold, but, when he sat down to a sumptuous meal, from soup to nuts, it transformed to highly indigestible gold as well. He was struck with horror when, at his touch, his priceless daughter went to $1,500.00 an ounce. Nicolas Poussin's (1594-1665) opus (Fig. 47), painted in 1629, portrays the contrite Midas entreating Bacchus to rescind what surely was the most questionable gift ever! The painting suggests a Temperance League cautionary tale, as everyone who is featured in the painting, including the kids, have passed out from an excess of demon drink.

Eros and Psyche. Psyche, the Greek and Roman goddess of the soul, was a world beauty who motivated a jealous Aphrodite (Roman: Venus) to commission her son Eros, the god of love (Roman: Cupid) to spear her with his arrow of ineluctable love at the sight of the most ugly creature in the world. The plot went awry when Eros was the first being Psyche saw and the soulful Eros fell in love with her. The depiction of that moment was beautifully rendered by Francois Gérard (1770-1837) in *Psyché et l'Amour*

(Fig. 48). The myth is more intricate than the painting shows, and there are countless versions of it in art and literature, but, most significantly and emblematically, Psyche – the soul – was joined in sacred wedlock with Eros – Love.

Fig. 48. Gérard. *Psyché et l'Amour*

A contemporary of poet Homer was Hesiod (active c. 700 BCE) who wrote *Theogony* (origin of the gods) and *Works and Days* (myths of Prometheus, Pandora and others) in which the evolution of the world is entwined with divine kings and queens who exploit the foibles and weaknesses of mortals. Some 600 years later, Apollodorus of Athens (c. 180-125 BCE) compiled the heroic legends in a work called the *Library of Pseudo-Apollodorus*. Mythological stories were further reinforced by lyric poets like Pindar of Thebes (c. 522-443 BCE) and Simonides of Ceos (c.556-468 BCE), playwrights Aeschylus (c. 525-455 BCE), Sophocles (c. 497-406 BCE), Euripides (c. 480-406 BCE) and Aristophanes (c. 446-386 BCE).

Fig. 49. Rinehart. *Latona with Apollo and Diana.*

Leto. Apollo and Artemis (Roman: Diana) were the offspring of Leto (Roman: Latona) and Zeus (Roman: Jupiter).[6] Hera was having none of it, and, to spite her profligate husband, forbade Leto to give birth on any land. Resourcefully, in one version of the myth, Leto delivered her babes on the floating island of Delos. *Latona with Apollo and Diana* (Fig. 49) was sculpted metaphorically as the goddess of motherhood and protector of children by William Rinehart (1825-1874). The twins bear a striking resemblance to Rinehart's *Sleeping Children* at the Yale museum.

Pandora. Zeus ordered the gods to create the first woman on earth as vengeance for Prometheus's deliverance of fire to the world. Each of the gods showered her with gifts. Zeus wickedly gave her a jar that contained every imaginable evil. When Pandora, unaware of its contents, opened the jar, all of the world's iniquities were released – save hope, which remained in the jar when Pandora sealed it. In the Cabanel painting of the opera singer, Christine Nilsson as Pandora (see Fig. 31), her hand is on the jar. The enigmatic smile on her lovely face keeps one guessing. Is she about to open the jar or close it?

Adonis and Aphrodite. There are so many subplots associated with the story of Adonis, the embodiment of male beauty, and Aphrodite, the goddess

50

of love. So many characters! – and jealousy, incest, intrigue, death, a return from death, a transformative change in nature. A straightforward focus on one aspect of the myth, as seen in Joachim Wtewael's (1566-1638) painting *Adonis and Aphrodite* (Fig. 50), seems the prudent approach to relate the tale of love and loss. The painting shows a besotted Aphrodite cozying up to a receptive Adonis. Eros, his body leaning against the goddess, is at the ready with an arrow that fires up love. The dogs in the painting allude to Adonis's love of the hunt, which was to be his undoing. Ignoring Aphrodite's warnings, he chased a wild boar into the forest and was gored to death (or was the animal the jealous god Ares in disguise as some say?). Legend has it that Aphrodite lovingly poured ambrosia on the fatal wound. It fell on droplets of his blood that turned into bright red anemones that continue to blossom.

Fig. 50. Wtewael. *Adonis and Aphrodite.*

Phaeton. Son of the sun god, Helios (Roman: Sol), Phaeton rode with his father in a chariot every day to give mortals a daily sunrise and a sunset. Phaeton begged his father to allow him to take the reins until Helios relented. Inexperienced, Phaeton lost control of the horses, and the chariot of fire plummeted to earth, scorching the savannas of Africa to create deserts and charring black the inhabitants' skin. The ill-tempered Zeus zapped him with a thunderbolt and killed him, but in Shakespearean fashion, he was 'cut into little stars'[7] as the constellation Auriga. The dramatic baroque painting, *Phaéton on the Chariot of Apollo* (Fig. 51) by Nicolas Bertin (1667-1736), depicts our hero just before the catastrophe.

Fig. 51. Bertin. *Phaéton on the Chariot of Apollo.*

Apollo and Daphne. The beautiful nymph Daphne spurned the advances of all men. An angry Eros (Roman: Cupid) pierced Apollo with his love inducing golden arrow, sending Apollo on a relentless chase after a fleeing Daphne through the woods. She prayed to the river god, Ladon, to be rid of Apollo, and he accommodatingly transformed her into a laurel tree. The romanticized painting, *Apollo and Daphne* (Fig. 52) by Paolo Veronese (1528-1588), captures the moment as Daphne sprouts branches and leaves from her head, hands and feet. Helpless to stop the transformation, a self-pitying Apollo stands beside her, thwarted and forlorn.

River god Ladon was the sea serpent cum dragon with one hundred heads who guarded the western reaches of the sea and the tree with the golden apples of the Hesperides. In labor eleven, Herakles defeated it. The Greeks had nearly 60 river gods, among them Carcinus, the giant crab who joined Hydra in attacking Herakles. When it died Hera placed it in the sky as a constellation and Hippocrates named the neoplastic disease after it – cancer.

Fig. 52. Veronese. *Apollo and Daphne.*

The Danaides. Against his wishes, the fifty daughters of Danaus married the fifty sons of his twin brother Aegyptus. There's nothing like keeping it in the family! Danaus ordered them to kill their husbands on the wedding night. All but one daughter complied. The others were condemned to the Sisyphean task of carrying water to fill a perforated basin for all eternity. In 1903, John William Waterhouse (1849-1917), who had a penchant for mythological paintings and pretty girls, painted an imaginative and strikingly colorful pre-Raphaelite rendition entitled simply *The Danaides* (Fig. 53).

Selene and Endymion. Ubaldo Gandolfi's (1728-1781) *Selene and Endymion* (Fig. 54), painted 1770, is now in the Los Angeles Museum of Art. Common to mythology, there are variations of the story, but this enchanting interpretation captured the essence of the myth in an irresistibly beautiful, chimerical composition. The moon goddess is decidedly moonstruck as the handsome shepherd boy, Endymion, the object of her ardor, dreams on and on and on. She had asked Zeus to keep him eternally youthful, and Zeus took her at her word. Be careful what you wish for, you

53

may get it. Zeus zapped Endymion into a sleep for eternity. Undeterred, Selene resourcefully managed to become pregnant fifty times and delivered all fifty girls.

Fig. 53. Waterhouse. *The Danaides.*

Hesiod's *Theogony* begins with *Chaos* – a black void – out of which *Gaia* (earth) materialized along with other gods such as *Eros* (love), Erebus (darkness) and *Tartarus* (abyss). *Gaia*, in a cosmic example of partheno-genesis, gave birth to *Uranus* (sky), who in turn committed incest with *Gaia*, giving birth to the Titans, one of which was *Cronus*. A wicked boy, he castrated his father, *Uranus*. *Cronus* married *Rhea* (more incest), and, fearing one of his offspring would do the same to him as he did to his father, he ate each newborn. Well, an infuriated *Rhea* managed to hide one child from him – *Zeus*!

Fig. 54. Gandolfi. *Selene and Endymion.*

Niobe. Niobe and Amphion, king of Thebes, had seven sons and seven daughters. At a ceremony to honor Leto, Niobe pompously boasted about her fourteen children to Leto's two. Leto took umbrage at the impudence of the comparison by a mere mortal to Leto's twins, the godly Apollo and Artemis, sired by Zeus. Leto's fury impelled her to show Niobe a thing or two – in this instance, fourteen things. She ordered Apollo to slay all seven of Niobe's sons, and Artemis to kill all of the girls. Niobe was inconsolable (as was Amphion, who, it is said, committed suicide). Zeus took pity on the wretch by turning her to stone to acquit her of emotion and dispel her anguish. He underestimated a mother's love, for, from a crevice in the stone poured an endless stream of grief stricken tears. The water testifies to Niobe's eternal sorrow, and it is said that to this day people say her image can be seen on a rock on Mount Siplyon, presumably with water streaming from it. Johann König's (1586-1642) *The Death of Niobe's Children* (Fig. 55), in the Louvre, portrays Apollo and Artemis committing the horrific massacre with bow and arrow, as the hapless Niobe looks on, arms raised in despair.

Fig. 55. Köing. *The Death of Niobe's Children.*

Alcyone and Ceyx. Alcyone, the daughter of the god of wind and Ceyx, the just and peaceful king of Trachis, deeply loved each other and were universally admired for their devotion. Sadly, their Halcyon days together were doomed when they began to playfully call each other "Hera" and "Zeus,' incurring the wrath of the cantankerous king of the gods. Thou shalt not take the name of Zeus in vain! The testy tyrant seethed until an opportunity for vengeance presented itself. When Ceyx sailed to Ionia to consult the oracle of Apollo, Zeus hurled a thunderbolt that triggered a powerful hurricane that wrecked the ship. Ceyx, with death imminent, prayed to the gods to be washed up on shore, in hopes of proper burial rites, essential for entrance into Hades, the underworld. Alcyone, unaware of her dearly loved husband's fate, waited in vain for his return. She prayed to Hera constantly as each day her fears compounded. Hera felt compassion for her, and charged Hypnos, the god and comforter of the aggrieved, to ameliorate her suffering. Hypnos instructed his gifted son, Morpheus, to conjure a vision of all that had happened to Ceyx. Desolate, Alcyone ran to the shore to her beloved's side. Once she had performed the last rites, she threw herself into the sea, to unite with him in the nether world. The Olympian gods were abashed by the tragic consequence of Zeus's injudicious and fatal reprimand and transformed the couple into Halcyon birds (kingfishers). Legend has it that Alcyone's father each year provides weeks of calm seas and breezeless weather so that the kingfishers can lay their eggs on the beach. A detail of the painting (Fig. 56) by Herbert James Draper (1863-1920) shows the beautiful Alcyone in grief by the seashore with two iconographic kingfishers hovering over her.

Fig. 56. Draper. *Halcyon* (detail).

Arachne. Arachne was a beautiful weaver who boasted about her skill, and, thinking none surpassed her talent, foolishly challenged Athena, the goddess of wisdom and crafts, to a contest. Athena punished her impudence by turning her into a spider, doubtless hoping her victim would produce a snarled web as she practiced her weaving forever more. Paolo Veronese's

57

(1528-1588) fresco, belies that outcome in his painting of Arachne (Fig. 57) as she admires a perfectly beautiful spider net. Score one for mortals! Originally in the Ducal Palace of Gubbio, it is now a part of the collection of New York's Metropolitan Museum of Art.

Fig 57. Veronese. *Arachne or Dialectic.*

Idas and Marpessa. Marpessa was promised to the suitor who won a chariot race. Poseidon, the god of the sea and sometimes thought to be the father of Idas, gave the youth a winged chariot that guaranteed he would win the race and the girl. When he went to claim his bride, Marpessa's possessive and tyrannical father, Evenus, would not release her, and Idas spirited her away. As they slept in a temple, Apollo made off with the very desirable damsel. Irate, Idas successfully pursued the pair, and he and Apollo engaged in an interminable and annoyingly noisy sword fight that irritated the gods. Zeus intervened and stopped the tussle. He commanded Marpessa to choose between Apollo and Idas. She shrewdly considered the pros and cons of the order. Apollo was a god and drop dead gorgeous who could offer everything one might desire. On the other hand, he was a god, and they were all known to be lascivious. Moreover, as a god, he was ageless, whereas, as a mortal, she would grow old and lose her beauty and appeal. That could leave her out in the cold! She evaluated Idas. True, he was a brutal warrior, and looked the part, but he loved her and would always protect her and be faithful. It was no contest. She chose Idas and sent the much abashed Apollo packing. The Greek vase (Fig. 58), crafted around 480 BCE, shows Zeus in the center separating Apollo and Artemis from Idas and Marpessa.

58

Fig. 58. Vase with Idas and Marpessa theme

The Naming of Athens. A half-man, half-snake creature, but also a king, Cecrops founded a beautiful city, which he called Cecropia. Each of the gods of Olympus longed to be the city's patron, with the city named after him/her. Athena and Poseidon were the most perseverant in vying for that privilege, and Zeus decided each should give a gift to the city and let king Cecrops decide which god would be granted the distinction. Poseidon struck a rock with his trident and created an artesian spring, thereby assuring the city always would have water, but the water of the God of the sea was salty. Athena planted an olive pit in the ground that blossomed into a olive tree that yielded food, oil and firewood, a gift to the city that would keep on giving, The olive branch was awarded to her by Cecrops, and the city was named Athens. A drawing made in 1896 by Karl Schwerzek (1848-1918) provided the groundwork for a model of the defunct west pediment of the Parthenon that depicted the naming of Athens (Fig. 59).

Cadmus. Cadmus was the king of Thebes who introduced the Phoenician alphabet to the Greeks. He was an adventurer whose travels began with a search for his sister Europa. His reputation for being fearless is borne out in Hendrik Goltzius's (1558-1617) dramatic, energized and beautiful composition that depicts Cadmus as he prepares to thrust his spear into the fearsome looking monster (Fig. 60).

Fig. 59. *The Naming of Athens* as depicted on the west pediment of the Parthenon (detail).

Fig. 60. Goltzius. *Cadmus slays the Dragon*

60

Fig. 61. Titian. *Sisyphus.*

Sisyphus. Sisyphus, king of Corinth, in some renditions of the myth, was a ruthless, avaricious, deceitful and murdering reprobate who, as a side-line, promoted navigation and commerce. When he killed tourists to Greece, he overstepped the mark by violating the Greek principle of *xenia*: hospitality, courtesy, generosity and shelter for all those far from home. He gravely offended Zeus, the protector of this code, who ordered Thanatos, the then god of death, to punish Sisyphus by restraining him with chains. The cunning degenerate tricked Thanatos and chained him instead. With Thanatos out of action, no one on earth could die – not the elderly, the suffering, or those wounded by Ares's troops who had been engaged in heated battle. The ensuing stalemate was frustratingly thwarting, so Ares freed Thanatos, and life – and death – resumed their normal cycles. Exasperated, Zeus, his order to punish Sisyphus yet to be implemented, manacled the menace himself and contrived a unique punishment without parole. He damned Sisyphus to daily thrust a boulder to the top of a hill, watch it topple back down, and roll it up again in an interminable process. Titian's (c. 1488-1576) painting of *Sisyphus* (c. 1548) (Fig. 61) broadens the legend's drama by depicting Sisyphus metaphorically in hell with hideous beasts lurking (one nipping at his feet), as fiery ejecta explode about him as he vainly hauls his massive burden up hill. The chiaroscuro of the background and the luminous light on the incredibly muscled figure of Sisyphus prefigures the works of Caravaggio, who admired Titian's work and had been taught by Simone Peterzano, who had studied with Titian.

Tantalus offered his son as a sacrifice to the gods. He butchered him, boiled his body parts until tender, and gave each of the gods a serving. Incredulous and repulsed by his inhuman, unnatural act, the gods put him in a unique penal colony, Tartarus, where he was doomed forever to stand in a pool of water beneath a fruit tree. Whenever he reached for a fruit, the branch rose out of reach, and whenever he bent for a drink, the water receded. Gioacchino Assereto's (1600-1649) *Tantalise* (Fig. 62), displayed his extraordinary skill in depicting anatomy, but, the figure contradicts the legend's consequences of the punishment inflicted on him, since he produced a painting with an extremely well-nourished Tantalus. Nevermind. Look at those muscles. Look at the foreshortening. Fabulous.

Fig. 62. Assereto. *Tantalise.*(1635).

Thanatos. (Roman: Mors). He was the son of Nyx, the goddess of night and Erebos, the god of darkness (and son of Chaos), and had a twin brother, Hypnos, the spirit of sleep. Although he was the personification of non-violent or peaceful death, he was, as death is, merciless and hated by gods and mortals. An extinguished torch is his attribute (Fig.181). His siblings were Geras (the spirit of old age), Oizys (goddess of misery and suffering), Moros (the god of doom and gloom), Apate (the personification of deceit), Momus (the spirit of blame, scorn, mockery), Eris (the goddess of chaos, discord, strife) and Nemesis (the god of retribution for hubris and arrogance). *Oi vey iz mir*, what a family!

Pegasus and Bellerophon. Pegasus, the magical winged white horse was thought, of all things, to have been born from the blood of Medusa's head. Bellerophon, son of Poseidon, slayer of monsters and legendarily a great hero, was commissioned to kill the fire breathing Chimera, whose characteristics were the head of a lion and tail of a dragon, and his favorite sport was to terrorize the people of Lycia. Polyidus advised enlisting Pegasus to get the job done. Bellerophon spent a long night in the temple making offerings to Athena beseeching help in capturing Pegasus, and she obliged him with the gift of a golden bridle. The following morning, Bellerophon sought Pegasus at the Peirene well he was known to frequent. He hid in the bushes until the horse knelt to drink, whereupon he hopped onto his back, slipped on the impressive bridle and took off. Bellerophon killed the Chimera and succeeded with other feats of valor that swelled his reputation as a hero – and his head. Arrogant and full of pride, he elected to dwell among the gods on Mount Olympus and flew Pegasus to the home of all the gods. Zeus, furious at his audacity, sent a gadfly to bite Pegasus, and Bellerophon tumbled off the legendary horse. Athena softened the ground for his fall, and he survived, but severely impaired and blind, and left to live the rest of his life in misery and isolation. Zeus kept the pony. Giovanni Battista Tiepolo (1696-1770) loved to paint skies (especially as murals on ceilings) – radiant blue skies, with luscious cotton-candy clouds. Worth risking a stiff neck to admire them. It has been said he was the greatest artist of the eighteenth century, noted for his spectacular theatrical rococo frescos óf ancient history and mythological themes. Pegasus was one of his favorite subjects, and he painted the myth of Bellerophon and Pegasus being repelled by the gods on Mount Olympus in a dazzling fresco measuring almost 9.7 by10.7 meters (32 by 35 feet). Tiepolo could do it all: perfect scale and composition, trompe l'oeil, skill in depicting anatomy in seemingly impossible positions – (that horse! those putti!) – rich color on sumptuous fabrics. Tiepolo was like Gulley Jimson in Joyce Cary's *The Horse's Mouth*, a blank wall or ceiling was an irresistible opportunity to paint yet another sky.

Fig. 63. Tiepolo. *Bellerophon on Pegasus* (detail).

Cassandra, daughter of king Priam and queen Hecuba of Troy, had been endowed with the power of prophesy by a lecherous Apollo, who had seduction in mind.   Having refused his advances, Apollo petulantly corrupted her gift so that no one would believe her prophesies. One version of the myth relates that Apollo, quite upset with her, spat into her mouth to inflict the curse. Evelyn de Morgan (1855-1919 painted Cassandra (Fig. 64) driven to the brink of madness as Troy burns in the background. Cassandra had told the Trojans it would happen, and, as usual, was spurned. It was enough to make her want to pull her hair out*

---

*They, in fact, call this condition trichotillomania. Another account of the story is that she fell asleep in an Asclepios temple (the ancients' version of a spa), and snakes licked her and whispered the gift of prophesy into her ears. This may be a clue that ophidiophobia drove her mad.

Fig. 64. de Morgan. *Cassandra's Madness.*

Narcissus. The handsome young Narcissus was the son of the river god Cephissus and the nymph Liriope. Proud and self-absorbed, he was incapable of loving others. Nemesis, the goddess of retribution, deplored his attitude and attracted him to a languid crystal pool. Narcissus looked into the water, saw his reflection and instantly fell in love, unaware it was merely his own image. Some think he stared at the image until he died; others that, when he bent to kiss the reflection, he fell into the water and drowned. Michelangelo Merisi da Caravaggio (1571-1610) brilliantly captured the boy's obsessive fixation with himself (Fig. 65). All of the characteristics of this genius were employed to produce an outstanding portrait with a narrative of immense depth and poignant drama: the light that floods in from the left; the chiaroscuro surrounding the figure; the anatomical accuracy; the brushwork that achieves the realism of the painting, seen most strikingly in the youth's hair and clothing. Caravaggio adroitly conveys an atmosphere of melancholy in his portrayal of Narcissus that elicits sympathy and pathos.

65

Fig. 65. Caravaggio. *Narcissus.*

Oedipus. The king of Thebes was the son of Laius and his wife, Jocasta. Laius learned of a prophesy that his son would kill him and marry his wife, and exposed Oedipus at birth to die. The infant was found and raised by king Polybus and queen Merope in Corinth. As a young man, Oedipus learned of the prophesy, but believed it referred to Polybus. To escape an ignoble fate, he left for Thebes, and on the way he met an old man on the road with whom he quarreled and killed. Upon his arrival in Thebes, controlled by the Sphinx, he was challenged with a riddle and solved it. His reward was the throne and the hand in marriage of the by now widowed queen Jocasta. After fathering four children with her, it was revealed that Jocasta was his mother and the man he killed was his father. Sophocles' drama of the tale is the definitive interpretation of the tragedy. Jocasta hanged herself and Oedipus blinded himself and went into exile. Unrivaled material for opera, Stravinsky wrote a popular opus based on the Greek play. Bénigne Gagneraux's (1756-1795) neoclassical painting, *Oedipus commends his children to the gods.* (Fig. 66) creates a drama, with Oedipus in the lead role as a despondent and resigned tragic figure surrounded by his grieving children and a supporting cast that reinforces the wretched and heartbreaking catastrophe that has befallen a noble man. Sigmund Freud (1856-1939) took out patents on these last two myths.

Fig. 66. Gagneraux. *Oedipus commends his children to the gods.*

Actaeon, was a Theban hero trained by a centaur. While hunting, he stumbled across Artemis naked and bathing. Unsurprisingly he lingered, unable to tear his eyes away from her. Once spotted by Artemis and her ladies in waiting, the infuriated Artemis warned him not to mutter a word or she would turn him into a deer. But. When Actaeon heard his dogs barking – all forty of them – he automatically called out to them. Poof! Now a deer, Actaeon became his dogs' prey, and, unable to outrun them, he was mauled to death. Talk about being in the wrong place at the wrong time! The fountain in the Palace of Caserta, Campania Italy, has a wonderful sculpture, the work of Paolo Persico (1729-1796), of the unfortunate Actaeon sprouting horns as the dogs attack him (Fig. 67).

The mythology of gods and mortals was famously retold around 8 BCE by Roman poet Ovid (43 BCE - 17 CE), in his *Metamorphoses*, which comprises 15 books that narrate over 250 tales. These can be grouped into stories of love, incest or seduction by a god on a mortal woman resulting in a heroic offspring, or into stories of punishment such as *Prometheus, Tantalus, Sisyphus, etc.*

Fig. 67. Persico. *Actaeon.* Fountain at the Palace of Caserta.

Twelve Labors of Hercules. (Greek: Herakles). In Greek mythology he was the son of Zeus and the mortal Alcmene. In a moment of madness induced by a jealous and vindictive Hera, Herakles killed his wife and sons. Restored to sanity, he was horrified by his actions and traveled to Delphi to seek atonement. Pythia told him to go and serve Eurystheus (who, with Hera, reviled Herakles), and, for twelve years perform very specific death defying feats: 1-slay the man-eating Nemean lion, 2-slay the Lernaean hydra, 3-capture the faster-than-a-speeding-bullet hind of Ceryneia, 4-bring back the Erymanthean boar, 5-clean the Augean stables (30 years' worth of muck, but with hydrologic inventiveness, Herakles diverted two rivers to scour them presto), 6-defeat the fierce and bronze-beaked Stymphalian birds, 7-capture the Cretan bull, 8-bring back the man-eating mares of Diomedes, 9-steal the girdle of Hippolyta, Queen of the Amazons, 10-steal the cattle of Geryon that were guarded by the two-headed dog Orthus, 11-gather the golden apples from the garden of the Hesperides,* 12-capture Cerberus, a three-headed cur and guardian of Hades. There are countless depictions of these labors mostly on Greek vases, mosaics and sculptures. As reliefs, they are found on sarcophagi, one example of which is Roman, 3rd century CE. The front panel shows nine labors (Fig. 68).

---

*Herakles didn't know where the garden was located. The sea god, Nereus directed him to Prometheus, who was most unfortunately incapacitated, as an eagle daily ate his liver. Herakles killed the eagle and released Prometheus, who, understandably much gratified, eagerly gave him directions to the garden.

Fig. 68. Roman sarcophagus *The Twelve Labors of Hercules.*

The most famous depiction of Herakles, now in the Museo Archeologico Nazionale, Naples, is the so called *Farnese Hercules* (Fig. 69) from the Farnese collection, by the Greek Glycon. It is a magnificent copy of the original sculpture by the great Lysippos of Sicyon, 4th century BCE. Colossal in size, it shows a weary Hercules/Herakles after the hero has completed his legendary twelve labors. The sculpture references two of those – the lion pelt on the club on which the figure leans and the three golden apples (held behind his back) from the garden of the Hesperides. The contrast between that hunk of a man and his exhausted expression and weary posture is fabulously executed. Herakles, incidentally, became a god and married the daughter of Zeus, the eternally young, Hebe, cup-bearer of the gods (Fig. 70).

Fig. 69. Farnese *Herakles.*   Fig. 70. Canova. *Hebe.*

A painting by Gregorio de Ferrari (1647-1726 describes the to the death *fracas* between Herakles and the half-giant Antaeus (Greek: Antnios), (Fig. 71) son of the earth goddess Gaia and Poseidon, whose indomitable strength had been granted him by his mother. The monster challenged all who he met to wrestling matches he always won, and thereafter he routinely killed the vanquished. He and Herakles encountered each other coincidently as Herakles headed back from Hesperides to Mycenae. As they wrestled, Herakles was continually thrown to the ground and he finally conjectured Antaeus was unassailable as long as his feet touched the earth. As they continued to scuffle, Herakles ensured his Antaeus' feet never touched the ground and his nefarious opponent's strength drained from his body, enabling Herakles to defeat and kill him.

Fig.71. De Ferrari. *Antaeus and Herakles.*

Judgment of Paris. A golden apple was offered as a prize to whoever was deemed the most beautiful goddess. Hera, Athena and Aphrodite were the contestants. Zeus declined to serve as judge and named the Trojan mortal, Paris, as judge. Bribes poured in: Hera offered to make Paris a king; Athena promised she would teach him all the skills of war; Aphrodite offered him the most beautiful woman in the world, Helen of Sparta. Paris took her up on it and awarded the apple to Aphrodite, absconded back to Troy with Helen, thereby inciting the Trojan War. In Rubens's depiction of the myth, Paris appears to take his time mulling over his decision, with the god Hermes looking on as the voluptuous trio flaunt their sumptuous silhouettes (Fig. 72).

Fig. 72. Rubens. *Judgment of Paris.*

Penelope. Penelope is the allegory of a chaste and faithful spouse. She was the wife of Odysseus and mother of Telemachus. Odysseus, soldiering in the Trojan War, was away from home for ten years. Many suitors tried to convince Penelope that Odysseus was long dead, never to return. She used many ruses to keep the suitors at bay, most famously weaving a burial shroud for her father-in-law. She promised she would make a choice once the shroud was finished, but every night she unraveled what she had woven

71

during the day. The Pre-Raphaelite painting from 1912 by John Waterhouse (1849-1917) depicts lovelorn suitors pining and proffering gifts as Penelope, seemingly oblivious to their presence, cunningly continues with her weaving (Fig. 73).

Fig. 73. Waterhouse. *Penelope and Suitors.*

Hephaestus and Aphrodite. (Roman: Vulcan and Venus) The son of Zeus and Hera, the god, Hephaestus, although strong, was born misshapen and lame. Zeus gave Aphrodite's hand in marriage to his son, but she soon strayed from the deformed, muscle-bound smithy who served as blacksmith to all the gods. She had an affair with Ares (Roman: Mars), the god of war. When Hephaestus learned of her betrayal, he sought revenge. As a great blacksmith, he was able to forge a virtually invisible metal net in which he ensnared the two lovers in the heat of passion in bed and assembled all the gods to expose their treachery and humiliate them. Floris Frans (1519-1570) painted a clueless Vulcan at work in his forge while Venus looks on (in the company of Cupid) and tellingly holds Mars' gear (Fig. 74).

God of war Ares, was the son of Zeus and Hera and one of the Twelve Olympian gods. He was the brute of war, ferocious and undisciplined, and, the antithesis of Athena who was deliberate, strategic and intelligent.

Fig. 74. Frans. *Venus and Vulcan at the Forge.*

Achilles was a client of Hephaestus who forged his armor to use in the Trojan War. Achilles was the mortal son of Thetis who longed to make her son immortal. As an infant, she dipped the infant Achilles into the River Styx, immersing his entire body except for the back part of his foot, which she held fast in her hand. Wouldn't you know it, that heel, Paris, pierced the one vulnerable spot on Achilles' body with a poisoned arrow and killed him. Paul Rubens painted Achilles as a trademark chubby child as his mother is about to immerse him in the fetid Styx (Fig. 75). Rich in iconography, one of the Fates, Lachesis, the measurer of the length of the string of life, is in the picture, as is Charon the ferryman. Pillar figures of Persephone and Hades, the goddess and god of the underworld, are on each side of the painting respectively, and the three headed Cerberus, who guards the entrance, lies in the foreground.

Cerberus, also known as the three-headed hound of Hades, guarded the gates of the underworld to prevent the shades of the dead from escaping. It was the twelfth labor of Hercules to capture Cerberus.

Fig. 75. Rubens. *Achilles Dipped into the Styx.*

Nine Muses. The goddesses of inspiration in arts, science and music, they were the children of Zeus and Mnemosyne. Their reputations endure as symbols of creativity. A 2nd century CE sarcophagus (Fig. 76) delightfully depicts them with their attributes: Calliope, the muse of epic poetry, holds a writing tablet; Thalia (See Charites), the muse of comedy and pastoral poetry, looks at a comic mask; Terpsichore, the muse of dance, has a lyre; Euterpe, the muse of lyric poetry, has a flute; Polyhymnia's veil identifies her as the muse of sacred poetry; Clio, the muse of history, holds a scroll; Erato, the inspiration for lyric poetry, plays a lyre, and Urania represents, with globe and compass, astronomy.

Mnemosyne was the Titan goddess of memory. Disguised as a shepherd, Zeus seduced her nine times – thus the nine muses – and true to his libertine reputation, he slept with Calliope who gave birth to Korybantes.

Fig. 76. Anon. *Muses sarcophagus.*

Nymphs. These were female spirits, young, agile and mischievous. There were hundreds of them, divided into Dryads the tree nymphs, Naiads the water nymphs, Nereids the sea nymphs, woodland creatures who were companions to Artemis and Pan, and nymphs of the underworld. The satyr Marsyas sometimes traveled with the woodland nymphs playing his pipes, and thought himself so accomplished, he foolishly challenged Apollo – the god of music. He lost the competition and was flayed. Antonio de Bellis (1616-1656) depicts Apollo in the act of delivering the poor satyr's comeuppance (Fig. 77).

Fig. 77. De Bellis. *The Flaying of Marsyas*

75

These mythological stories comprise the most popularly depicted Greek myths, many of which became part of the canon of Roman mythology. For this reason, we retained the artists' Roman god titles artists used in their paintings. There are elements of mythology not associated with a particularly great story, yet have elements so charming, beautiful, fantastical or mysterious that artists through the centuries chose to depict them. The following are such examples.

Charites. Known as the Three Graces in the Western world, they personify beauty, charm, and creativity. They were the daughters of Zeus, and goddesses in their own right. Euphrosyne was the goddess of joy; Thalia, of comedy, and Aglaea, of beauty. They bestowed their attributes on the worthy, but mostly spent their time attending to Aphrodite and Eros and dancing to Apollo's music with Nymphs and Muses. One could spend hours, spellbound and in awe, looking at Antonio Canova's (1757-1822) neoclassical sculpture of the *Three Graces* that so exquisitely captures their elegance and beauty (Fig. 78).

Fig. 78. Canova. *Three Graces*

76

Centaurs. Beastly half man, half horse, they were children of Ixion, king of the Lapiths and Nephele, a cloud in Hera's image. In the main they were wild and violent and commonly depicted at war with the Lapiths. One of the Centaurs, unrelated to the bad hombres, was Chiron. He was known as a physician, astrologer and oracle. Gentle, kind, intelligent and caring, he tutored, among others, Asclepius, and taught Achilles to play the harp. Legendarily, Herakles accidentally wounded the centaur with a Hydra poisoned arrow, inducing intractable pain on the much-loved Chiron, who languished for days before he died. In another version of the story Herakles appealed to Zeus to release Prometheus; Zeus acquiesced on condition someone take his place. Chiron nobly offered himself. In any take on the myth, Chiron still emerges as a heroic figure granted the honor of a place in the firmament as a constellation.

Fig. 79. Anon. *Chiron instructs the young Achilles.*

Most mythology derived from the Greeks. Roman Virgil's *The Aeneid* told by the hero, Aeneas, is the classic example. The saga had first been recounted by the Greek, Homer, in *The Iliad*. Western artists who focused on mythological themes from the 16th through 19th centuries used the Roman versions as their sources. Of the limited original Roman mythology, a small number, frequently depicted, were popular.

77

♣

Laocoön. As told by the poet Virgil (70-19 BCE) in the *Aeneid,* Laocoön was a prophet and Trojan priest who tried to expose the Greek army's subterfuge to gain entry into the city in a wooden horse, and pleaded with authorities to leave it on the beach outside the city gates. Athena, protector of the Greeks, punished Laocoön and his sons by having the giant sea serpents Porces and Chariboea attack and kill them. In another version of the myth, Laocoön, ever the victim, was punished for breaking his promise of celibacy to Apollo. A famed sculpture of Laocoön and his sons *in extremis,* excavated in 1506 and placed in the Vatican museum, shows them agonizingly coiled in the serpents' tentacles. Many copies exist of this extraordinary sculpture that displays exceptional human anatomy, conveys powerful physical strength and psychic drama, and portrays realism and immediacy about Laocoön and his sons' ordeal. It is not known for certain who sculpted the piece, but Pliny the Elder (23-79 CE) named three Rhodesians, Agesander, Athenodorus and Polydorus as collaborators.

Fig. 80. Anonymous. *The Laocoön.*

78

Romulus and Remus. The most celebrated legendary twins in history, immortalized in stone in Rome, the city they are said to have founded. Born of Rhea Silvia, daughter of King Numitor of Alba Longa and the god Mars, their grand-uncle, having slain Numitor, ordered R & R drowned in the Tiber River. The babes miraculously survived on the shore of the river close by a sacred fig tree. They were rescued by a wolf, sacred to Mars, who suckled the infants until a shepherd and his wife – Faustulus and Acca – found and fostered them. As adults they learned of Amulius' treachery, and waged war against him, killing him and reinstating Numitor to power. They returned to the seven hills where they had been nurtured, and Romulus chose the Palatine Hill as the settlement's site and built a wall around it. Remus mocked his brother's belief in the impenetrability of the settlement and leaped over the wall. In raging pursuit, Romulus met up with Remus and killed him, and thereafter gave warning to anyone who dared oppose him. The new city of Rome – Romulus's homage to himself – grew, as Romulus encouraged immigrants – male fugitives and exiles – to settle there. The notable dearth of the fair sex prompted Romulus to negotiate for brides in nearby communities, but was rebuffed by respectable townships unwilling to give their daughters in marriage to thugs. Romulus plotted to force the issue and invited neighbors, mostly Sabines, to a festival. At his command, a predatory rape of the Sabine women ensued. All attempts to recover the women, including militant actions, failed, and Rome, soon with a multitude of children that had been propagated, prevailed and, as all know, grew into the mightiest empire in the Western world. And Romulus? In time he was worshiped by the Romans as the god Quirinus.

Fig. 81. *Romulus and Remus.*

Rape of the Sabines. Circa 750 BCE has been established as the purported time of the abduction. The story's drama was the perfect vehicle for Renaissance artists, whose passion was to perfect the depiction of the human form, and an endless number of contorted human torsos of terrorized women and rapacious men were committed to canvasses. As salacious scandals go, this one aroused a tremendous amount of interest, and was a very popular

79

theme with artists. Pietro da Cortona's (1596-1669) allegorical painting set in an idyllic glade captures, in a theatrically inspired moment worthy of a proscenium stage, the bewilderment and terror of the abduction as it is in progress as the triumphant Romulus crows in the background.

Fig. 82. Cortona. *Rape of the Sabines.*

Lucretia. Historians concede Lucretia was a virtuous Roman matron who committed suicide in 510 BCE after having been raped by the son of a despotic Etruscan king, Tarquinius Superbus. Roman historians Pictor and Livy wrote extensively about the tragedy. The details of the episode incited the population to war that resulted in the transition of Rome from a kingdom to a republic. The mythologized figure of Lucretia has been depicted in scores of paintings that portray her in the act of stabbing herself. The baroque version here is by Ludovico Mazzanti (1686-1775) (Fig. 83). The legend of Lucretia struck a chord through millennia. In addition to over one hundred known paintings, she is well known in literature: in Augustine of Hippo's (354-430) *City of God*, Dante Alighieri's (1265-1321) Canto IV of the *Inferno*, Geoffrey Chaucer's (1343-1400) *The Legend of Good Women*, Andre Obey's (1892-1975) *Le Viol de Lucrèce* and Shakespeare's *The Rape of Lucrece*. There was even an opera written about the distressing tale as recently as 1946, by Benjamin Britten (1913-1976), titled *The Rape of Lucretia.*

Fig. 83. Mazzanti. *Lucretia*

Mithras. Mithranism was a secret Roman cult from the 1st through the 4th century CE, tolerated because it strongly supported the emperor. The cult may have had roots in Persia, although most historians agree there is little evidence of that. In Rome, the majority of the worshipers of Mithras (perhaps from Mithra, the Persian god of friendship and order), were originally members of Roman military legions, which would account for traces of the cult throughout Italy and elsewhere. As the cult grew, freed slaves joined its members, with the caveat no women need apply. Meeting places for worship were generally underground, and, in addition to the majority of the more than 200 Mithras underground temples that have been found in Italy and along the Danube, there have also been archeological finds in Syria and Britain. Common to all of the altars in the temples were reliefs of Mithras slaying a sacred bull in what was believed to be a sacrificial act, with attendant symbolic emblems of the sun, moon and stars, all astrological references. These representations are so ubiquitous, a modern term, tauroctony, was coined to reference them. Beyond that, little is known about the cult's beliefs and rituals. Typically Mithras is depicted in a Phrygian hat as he stabs the bull, severing its neck vessels, while a dog and snake lick the flowing blood. An outstanding exemplary sculpture is in the British Museum (Fig. 84).

Fig. 84. *Mithras.*

Cybele. A Phrygian (now central and western Anatolia), goddess of fertility and all nature, abundance and the harvest, was usurped by Roman votaries as their own goddess, the great mother – *Mater Magna.* She was most fervently worshiped during the 2nd Punic War (218-201 BCE) when war, famine and Hannibal's threatening daring as he crossed the Alps on elephants scared the bejesus out of the Romans. Panicked, and staring defeat and ruin in the face, they plied Cybele with incessant prayers to save them. Cybele's attributes are a cornucopia, a lion at her feet and a pinecone – and yes, she was as tough as the sculpture suggests! (Fig. 85)

Fig. 85. *Cybele.*

82

♣

Within the sphere of allegorical and mythological painting, there exists a parallel space where bible themes and mythology are analogous. After the 15th century there were thousands of paintings that filled museums all over the world with storybook depictions of Adam and Eve, Cain and Able, Abraham's sacrifice, Susanna and the Elders, Salome and John Baptist, Judith and Holofernes, Tobias and the Angel, Esther before Ahasuerus and Joseph and Potiphar's Wife. From the New Testament, almost every moment of Christ's life on earth was depicted, from before he was born as a fetus to his wanderings after the resurrection. There are countless paintings of the Annunciation, the Visitation, the Nativity, the Three Magi, the Circumcision – and mind you, they refer to events before his first birthday! There's an endless series of Madonna and Infant paintings and the episode of Jesus and the Elders in the temple. Thereafter, he disappeared – in the New Testament and in art, until he surfaced again in the period of his ministry, arrest, passion, death, and resurrection. His mother Mary was honored and celebrated by countless artists in her own right. She was portrayed even in death. Her assumption into heaven, which was not declared doctrine until 1950, has been a topos of literature and depiction since 600 CE!

These themes were so common in art, there's no need to beat the dead horse. Adams and Eves on museum walls abound as poster children for the Book of Genesis, as do nativity scenes celebrating Christmas in museum after museum. It is enough to say that the decollations of John the Baptist and Holofernes were such popular themes, the pair lost their heads more times than those unfortunates whom Madame Guillotine axed during France's Reign of Terror. But Susanna and the Elders, Tobias and the Angel, the fetal Jesus, Christ post-resurrection and the death of the Virgin are interesting examples of biblical stories that have been depicted with the size, scale and gravitas seen in great mythological representations.

The story of Susanna and the Elders is from the book of Daniel. Protestants believe it to be apocryphal. The Church of England regards it as an edifying tale. In any case, it tells the story of how Susanna, bathing and attending to her toiletries, is spied on by two lecherous elders. They threaten to accuse her of sexual improprieties if she does not satisfy their lust. Daniel saves the day – and Susanna – by having the elders' claim discredited. The tale captured the imaginations of many artists, all of whom were eager for opportunities to depict the nude body. Of the many painted by some of the world's greatest artists, we chose to show the interpretation by Rubens, who liked the theme so much, he painted six different versions (Fig. 86).

83

Fig. 86. Rubens. *Susanna and the Elders.*

Tobias and the Angel, from the apocryphal book of Tobit, depicts the moment when the angel Raphael, Tobit's son Tobias at his side, heals Tobit's blindness with the heart, liver and gall bladder of a fish. The beautiful, colorful composition is by Simon van Amersfoort (1550-1630). (Fig. 87).

Jesus in fetal form was a topos in 12th and 13th century frescoes – a purely artistic fancy not based on scriptural references. The painting by Marx Reichlich (1460-1520), with its classical trappings and colorful garb contemporary to the times, shows the meeting of Mary and her cousin Elizabeth – mother of John the Baptist. The tiny Jesus is shown *in utero* with his hand raised in the iconic conceit of a blessing as he greets his cousin, John (of John the Baptist fame), also a fetus, kneels in adoring acknowledgement of Jesus' divinity (Fig. 88).

Fig. 87. Amersfoort. *Tobias and the Angel.*

Fig. 88. Reichlich. *The Visitation* and detail.

The three paintings here are all by Michelangelo Merisi da Caravaggio (1571-1610).[8] Two are post-resurrection themes: the doubtful Thomas and the Supper at Emmaus. John 20: 24 told the story of Thomas who would not believe in the resurrection of Jesus until he personally saw and touched his wounds. Caravaggio's technique is stamped all over both paintings: chiaroscuro, light blazing in from the left, realistic lifelike figures of the principals, energy, a sense of motion and drama, all marks of the master's touch. His signature method had huge influence, leading to a cadre of painters known as the *Caravaggisti*. Compositionally, in *The Incredulity of Thomas* (Fig. 89), the bent over apostles form two triangles that sweep the eye to the wound being probed by Thomas. Their expressions heighten the drama of the narrative, leaving the viewer with no doubt that doubting Thomas was convinced it was the risen Christ. Luke, 24: 13, related how Jesus appeared among them, initially unrecognized, at the *Supper at Emmaus* (Fig. 90). The painting, with all of the aforementioned Caravaggio hallmark techniques, captures on canvas the moment when the stunned disciples grasp the identity of the visitor.

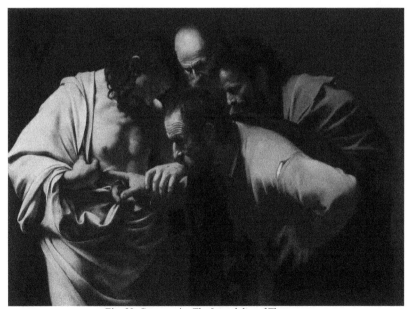

Fig. 89. Caravaggio. *The Incredulity of Thomas*

Fig. 90. Caravaggio. *Supper at Emmaus.*

The Death of a Virgin (Fig. 91), commissioned for the Carmelite church Santa Maria della Scala in Rome, was completed around 1606. The painting was rejected as unworthy of a portrayal of the mother of God and, in general, was much criticized. Rubens considered it Caravaggio's greatest work and convinced the Duke of Mantua to buy it. (Otherwise, we hypothesize the work might have been burned as scandalous and sacrilegious.) Critic André Félibien in 1696 remarked the ignoble looking body of the Virgin looked like a distended drowned woman,* but the comment disregards the naturalism and realism of the Caravaggio style. Ever the maverick, Caravaggio eschewed most of traditional Catholic iconography, conceding to Catholic convention only by robing Mary in a trademark red gown and a wire thin, barely visible, halo around Mary's head, we presume for the purpose to identify his subject. The painting is truly monumental (1.8 by 2.7 meters (6 by 9 feet), with a theatrical expanse of drapery (a well known pagan death iconoclass) that crowns the painting (and incidentally echoes Mary's red dress; a clever device that pulls the eye to the dead saint, as does the light on the tight group of nearly life size

*It is said the model for Mary was Caravaggio's mistress, a prostitute, not a drowned woman pulled from the Tiber River.

87

mourners who crowd the scene. Unidentifiable, the apostles in the scene are reminiscent of the ancient Roman *conclamatio*. They dramatically express the anguish of their loss as they hover at the base of a simple covered table on which Mary lies, some with faces obscured, others with hands covering their woeful faces. Encroaching light from the left passes over them and bursts into brilliance on the figure of Mary, highlighting the importance of the subject. She lies in death in an unconventional position, her complexion pallid, her arm flaccidly extended, abdomen distended, feet puffy, unlike any representation of Mary ever before painted. Where's her finery, the apotheosis, the reverence? Is that Mary Magdalene as a classic personified image of grief sitting beside her? The painting's power derives, in addition to the above related observations, from the stark, almost photographic, realism and the never before depicted humanity of Mary.

In Eastern Christianity, the Dormition of the Theotokos (Latin: *Mater Dei*) – the death of the Virgin – was a fundamental topos of belief and depiction. It was said that Mary went to live in the house of the apostle John in Jerusalem. There, Archangel Gabriel, who had announced she would be the mother of Jesus, appeared to her again, and this time and revealed that her death would occur in three days. Shortly the twelve apostles all gathered miraculously to witness her death and apotheosis into heaven. However, in Roman Catholicism, as the doctrine of the Assumption assumed import, the depictions gradually disappeared.

Fig. 91. Caravaggio. *The Death of a Virgin.*

Footnotes: Chapter Two

1. The debt to the Arab world in preserving classic Greek and Roman knowledge is inestimable. In the 5th century, the residue of Roman power was centered in Constantinople, but the focus by that time was on Christian themes. Pagans and their beliefs, knowledge, legends and writings, including that of the scholarly Greeks, were defiled. Christian Emperor Justinian I expelled important pagan philosophers who had been intellectually formed by the works of Greek and Roman civilizations. The exiles went to Persia and took with them all of the classic scholarship in their possession. Once the School of Plato in Athens collapsed a century later in 529, theirs was the only remaining source of Greek and Roman erudition. It was to remain so for centuries. In parts of Persia, Egypt and Syria, Syriac, a late dialect of Aramaic, was the *lingua franca* of pedagogy, and initially the writings of Greece and Rome were translated into Syriac. The Arab conquest of the 8th century engulfed the Syriac speaking world and an Arabic Empire emerged with absolute power. Its capitol in time was moved from Damascus to Baghdad in 762. Eastern scholars flourished under the Caliphs (c.749-1258) who, by edict, sanctioned the translation, from Syriac into Arabic, of Greek and Roman canons. An arbitrary decree, made for political expediency, the edict empowered the preservation of classical knowledge for all time, and the Arabic Empire became the caretaker of the classics that eventually were reintroduced into Western cultures: the works of Galen and the wisdom of Hippocrates, the philosophy and teleology of Aristotle, the dramas of Euripides, Aeschylus and Aristophanes, the poetry of Homer, Virgil and others, the astronomy of Thales and Apollonius and the mathematics of Pythagoras, Archimedes and Euclid. The Aristotelian belief in a purposeful divine creator – Aristotelian philosophy in general – was but one aspect of learning these monarchs encouraged, as new science and all of Greek classic works were promoted and studied, with scholars clamoring for more Greek knowledge – to become *sapientia et scientia*.

   The great Translation Movement that began in the 8th century continued for centuries. The transcriptions from Greek into Syriac and into Arabic, would in time refer to the translation of texts from Arabic back into Latin that reintroduced classical wisdom to the Western world. It constitutes the theme of "How the Arabs saved western civilization." (See Colón and Colón, *Tincture of Time*).

2. Cahill, Thomas. *How the Irish Saved Civilization.* New York: Talese, 1995.

3. It seems Pope Paul escorted his master of ceremonies, Biagio da Cesena to view the fresco, and Biagio opined that the large number of nudes in the work better belonged in a public bath, not a sacred painting. Michelangelo, it is said, took revenge by painting Biagio as Minos with the devil's serpent in fellatio. According to commentator Lodovico Domenischi (1564), when Biagio complained, Paul III responded, "M. Biagio, you know that I have power from God in heaven and on earth, but my authority does not extend into hell, so you will have to be patient since I am not able to free you from there."

4. Girolamo Savonarola (1452-1498) was a Florentine Dominican reformer and apocalyptic preacher who advocated a paranoid and extreme Puritanism. He is remembered for his inquisitorial bent, his disdain of papal authority and theatrical bonfire of the vanities in which the citizens of Florence willingly or not burned books, art, mirrors, cosmetics – anything with vanity connotations. Seeing Botticelli's pagan themes and nudity must have made him nuts.

5. Nuland, Sherwin B. *Leonardo da Vinci.* New York: Penguin Group, 2000. p. 75.

6. The family tree of Leto can be found on p. 243. Note the remarkable amount of sanctioned incest and some of Zeus's extramarital activities (in red text).

7. 'When he shall die, Take him and cut him out in little stars, And he will make the face of heaven so fine, That all the world will be in love with night, And pay no worship to the garish sun.' *Romeo and Juliet*, Act 3, Scene 2.

8. Although his body of work is small – some forty paintings by strict autographers and perhaps ten to twelve more by less demanding experts – Michelangelo Merisi da Caravaggio (1571-1610) and his *oeuvre* were a critical and influential cynosure for artists throughout Europe for centuries. Those influenced by him represent the artistic genius of a continent: von Honthorst, ter Burgghen, Rubens, Carracci, Reni, Guercino, Zurbarán, Ribera, Velázquez, de la Tour and Vouet, to name but a few. The dichotomy between the artist and his nature is striking and paradoxical. His private comportment earned him an unsavory reputation in his time as one whose disposition and temperament prompted frankly criminal behavior. His name appears in Roman police records for petty offences on a regular basis. The intercessions of his various patrons usually rescued him from official sanctions. In 1606, however, he killed Ranuccio Tomassoni in a duel over a tennis match and was forced to flee Rome. In 1610, Cardinal Ferdinando Gonzaga arranged an absolution for the murder of Tomassoni that would

allow Caravaggio to return to Rome. On his way to receive the pardon from Pope Paul V, Caravaggio contracted a fever in Porto Ercole. It was most likely tertian malaria, endemic in coastal 16th to 18th century Italy. He died in just a few days, on 18 July 1610, before receiving his pardon, but not before leaving his indelible mark on Europe's Baroque age: *Tenebrism*, the most imitated of Caravaggio's techniques that used sharp chiaroscuro, in which darkness predominates and enhances drama and there are pronounced contrasts of light and dark.

We're made so that we love
First when see them painted, things we
        passed
Perhaps a hundred times nor care to see;
And so they are better, painted – better to us,
Which is the same thing. Art was given for that.

Robert Browning (1812-1889) in *Fra Lippo Lippi*

Chapter Three: Let's go Dutch

A unique iconography emerged in Holland during the 17th century, consequent to the Reformation of the century before, its origins fueled by papal shenanigans. The self-indulging Medici Pope Leo X (1475-1521) had emptied Church coffers, thwarting Leo's wish to build a new church in Rome – a basilica, in fact. It was yet another of his extravagant whims, and it would be costly. Leo resourcefully devised a scheme to sell sin forgiving indulgences that, for a fee, eradicated sins. It was, for the faithful, an express ticket to heaven. For the genuinely devout, it was the last straw. That was especially true for the German Augustinian priest, Martin Luther (1483-1546), who as legend has it, in 1517 marched to the entrance of All Saints Church in Wittenberg, Germany, took a hammer and nailed his revolutionary 95 item manifesto on the door. With each hammer blow, a seismic shock convulsed Western society. Although a myth – Luther actually sent his thesis to his archbishop, Albert of Mainz (1490-1545) – the quake image holds, as the Reformation forever changed the forms of Christian worship. Luther's document expounded two basic tenets regarding the Faith that were to have an impact on art: the bible is the authoritative word, not church officials, and salvation comes through deeds. Forgiveness for sins was bestowed by God, not popes. In addition to condemning the sale of indulgences, the thesis denounced the nepotism, simony, and usury rampant in the Vatican. The schism between the northern European countries and the Church in Rome was irreparable. Protestantism, as several sects of beliefs – Lutheran, Calvinist, Anabaptist, and, in time, Anglican – drew countless numbers into their fold. Their canon was the Bible. Images, considered idolatrous, were ejected from all their churches. Pulpits supplanted altars. Paintings and statues disappeared from churches, viewed as objects of blasphemous veneration. There was no place for statues of saints in a house of worship and a Christian version of the Roman *damnatio memoriae* played out. The movement did not proceed smoothly. There were riots in many cities, most notoriously during the Dutch summer of 1566 when the *beeldenstorm* smashed and splintered Catholic church interiors. Statues and paintings were burned, stained-glass windows shattered and architectural reliefs on buildings defaced.

Political leaders, long subjugated by the power in Rome, welcomed the opportunity to undermine the tyrannical and corrupt Catholic institution. Oppositional forces during Spain's war against the Netherlands enabled the acquisition of both the property and immense wealth of the Roman Catholic Church. Henry VIII (1491-1547), self proclaimed Supreme Head of the Church, dissolved more than 900 monasteries, priories and convents (1536-1541) and displaced twelve thousand clergy, monks and nuns; he destroyed or sold their religious artifacts, seized their assets and melted golden reliquaries – a financial bonanza that funded Henry's foreign wars. It was the most radical of Reformation events, despite Henry's continued assertion he was Catholic. Two of his three progeny protested otherwise. In any case, churches became aniconic, and the market for religious depictions was defunct. Although there were continued requests in the private sector for *fijnschilder* jewels of devotional art in homes, patronage for artists on the grand scale came from those who entertained their preferences for historical and honorific paintings, portraits, still lifes, *vanitas* and morality genre works. A completely new iconography was the consequence, with an amalgam of reformation values, folklore, dictums, maxims and emblems. Genre still life floral paintings come to mind as examples of having embedded in them the concept of God's hand evident in all things, with nothing unworthy of depiction. Scrupulously detailed, richly colored, compositionally perfect paintings of flowers and all of *vita naturalis*, blemishes and imperfections included, were portrayed. Their beauty always inferred that decay was just around the corner. Everyday objects and actions highlighted such themes in the Dutch Golden Age in art of the Baroque from mid 16th through the 17th centuries. These fundamentals gradually spread throughout Europe, but nowhere with the elegance, exactitude and artistic grace of Dutch artists.

The people of the Netherlands of the 17th century were the richest per capita in the whole of Europe. They had money to spare, and the fashion was to use it on art. Most paintings commissioned were for display in the home, with the exception of the usually massive in scope and size honorifics such as Rembrandt's *The Night Watch* and the *Anatomy Lesson of Doctor Tulp* and heralded national themes of war and conquest. Portraits were the rage, and sitters expected a good likeness, with the self-perceived virtues within them on view in various facets underscored in the work. Some artists merely revealed the sitter's age, or the year the work was painted. Wealth was evident from the refinement of costumes, background furnishings and drapery, and subjects' occupations were obvious by the accouterments seen in the painting. The main point is that all art served as a moral compass, however it was presented.

Dutch painters were part of guilds, one of which was the Guild of St. Luke, named for the Evangelist, patron of artists. Guilds had traditional apprenticeships and controlled the production and sale of art works. It operated within a market system that catered to the rich and, to a degree, the merchant class; and to all, aimed to display their highly variable individual tastes. The consequence was an evolution of specialized categories of art that included private devotional art, domestic social life, landscapes, townscapes, market scenes, maritime themes, still lifes of flowers, animals and fruit – with glasses of wine, silver goblets, nuts and even an insect on the canvas now and then – and everyday household objects. Additionally, there were the aforementioned depictions of national and historical interest and honorifics; and, unique to the Dutch and Flemish, a genre of humorous *tronies,* depictions of unique physiognomy of ordinary individuals with exaggerated expressions or attitudes that had no narrative content.

Scholars estimate that during the Dutch Golden Age, over five million paintings were produced (less than two percent have survived), so it follows there must have been scores of artists, probably thousands. Of those, most art sources list approximately four hundred of the most prominent of the period. Mentioned here are a mere handful, with the intention to focus on the unique iconography of the period. In the post-Reformation world that eschewed explicit symbols of religion, there were artistic expressions of biblical scenes and moral lessons. Artists were inspired by the work of Giovanni Campani (c.1560-1620), better known as Cesare Ripa, who wrote *Iconologia overo Descrittione Dell'imagini Universali cavate dall'Antichità et da altri luoghi* (1593). It is an illustrated work that compiled, with definitions and depictions, more than seven hundred emblems that consisted of individual images, each of which connoted a moral concept accompanied by an epigram, caption and an explanatory verse. The virtues and conceits depicted in Ripa's *Iconologia* are self-explanatory, as are those in *Hospitalita*, whose welcoming generosity was represented by the cornucopia she holds in her hand as due homage to her is being given by Santiago de Compostela (which, incidentally, features his conceit, the scallop, on his shoulder (Fig. 92). Ripa worked for Cardinal Anton Maria Salvati (1537-1642) as a cook and butler, and, in moments of leisure, he wrote his *Iconologia,* arranging all entries (Egyptian, Greek and Roman thematic elements) alphabetically. It was a highly successful work, with nine Italian editions and eight translations into French, Dutch, German and English. Ripa was knighted for his opus.

H O S P I T A L I T A.

V N A belliffima donna , hauerà con l'v_a
fronte d'vn cerchio d'oro tutto contefto
di prenofiffime gioie,& i capelli faranno bion-
di,& ricciuti,con vagha & belliffima accoocia
tura,farà d'età virile con faccia allegra, & ri-

dentre,ftarà con le braccia aperte in atto di rice
uere altrui,con la deftra mano terrà vn Cornucopia con dimoftratione di votarlo,il quale fra
pieno di fpighe di grano,vue,frutte diuerfe_,,
danari,& altre cofe appartinere all'vfo huma-

Fig. 92. Ripa. *Hospitalita* from *Iconologia*.

Perhaps the artworks most immediately envisaged with the mention of Dutch paintings are the endearing intimate and captivating social genre paintings. For the most part they share several characteristics: aspects of everyday life of anonymous subjects whose occupations are identifiable. Domestic scenes were realistic, romanticized or invented, sentimental, instructive or moralizing; they served as a medium in which artists displayed unique technical skills. In addition to composition and perspective, their works displayed masterful proficiency in narratives that conveyed the essence of the theme and subjects' emotions. Their technique in rendering the sheen and tactual feel of fabrics was exemplary. Gerard ter Borch's (1617-1681) *A Lady at Her Toilet* is a fine example (Fig. 93) (It was a theme painted several times by ter Borch, with slight distinguishing differences). The painting of a richly outfitted boudoir shows an arresting standing figure dressed in a magnificent blue and white satin gown attended by a page and a maidservant, and, sets the scene for mystery. Pensive, with an enigmatic expression, the lady toys with her ring, as a page, seemingly tremulous, extends a flagon of perhaps perfumed water. The maid who tends to her gown is outside of the narrative framework, but her presence calls attention to the exquisite rendering of the lady's satin gown. A cursory look and it appears a simple scene, but, on closer inspection, it is loaded with drama and psychological depth that invites questions: why does she look so preoccupied? Does it have something to do with ambiguous feelings about the man who gave her the ring? Does the mirror, long a symbol of vanity, deliberately depict an improbable likeness, due to the reflection's angle? Or does it reflect something false in her nature? Does it reflect sadness? What do the doused candles imply? Dutch iconography would suggest the ephemeral nature of life. Here the artist's work tempts a darker interpretation. A lover's deceit, perhaps? Or second thoughts about the guy? The beauty and skill of the painting is not in question, Ter Borch subtly demands the viewer go beyond admiration of his work to consider psychological and moral issues with regard to the complexity of human experience and take to heart the universally known conceit of *vanitas* – life is transient and earthly pleasures are ephemeral. Ter Borch, Jan Vermeer (1623-1675), Gabriel Metsu (1629-1667) and Pieter de Hooch (1627-1683) all painted exceptional – similar – *scènes intimes* that lure the viewer into a labyrinth of complex human emotions.

Fig. 93. ter Borch. *A Lady at her Toilet.*

Tavern life was a very popular theme depicted by esteemed artists such as Adriaen van Ostade (1610-1685), Jan Steen (1625-1679), Gerrit Dou (1613-1675), Dirck Hals (1591-1656) and Adriaen Brouwer (1605-1638). Presented with humor, they all have an iconographic moral message, such as in Brouwer's *Tavern Scene* (Fig. 94). On the left, a drunken lout sits, legs spread apart, his hand reprehensibly groping underneath the gown of the woman next to him, his spilt beer a reflection of his excess. The woman tries to push his hand away, simultaneously pulls his hair and elicits a wince (The expression on her face looks like half hearted indignation, if you want our opinion). Three men stand on the right with lecherous looking laughs around him to egg him on. Voyeuristic faces leer from a small window. In contrast, two men seated in the foreground in animated conversation exemplify proper tavern comportment, indifferent to the somewhat reprehensible behavior going on around them. Van Ostade's younger brother Isack (1621-1649), although primarily remembered for his winter landscapes, also depicted tavern scenes, coarse images with mischievous scatological humor that depict subjects urinating or defecating and carcasses of cows or pigs being cleaned after having been butchered.

Fig. 94. Brouwer. *Tavern Scene.*

Jan Steen (1626-1679) is the master of emblematic narratives in crowded canvasses filled with myriad examples of *la comédie humaine*, rich in color and composition that collectively delivered powerful as well as engaging moral messages. He was a story teller, a Catholic in Calvinistic country, who moralized with humor and the genius of an outstandingly skilled artist. *Beware of Luxury* (Fig. 95) documents mayhem in a domestic household one would more likely expect to see in a tavern. Alcohol appears to be the major culprit responsible, but Steen's indictment goes well beyond a single cause. The chaos in the picture is littered with symbols that reinforce its title: *In weelde siet tot,* from a Dutch proverb that foresees change in good fortune in a home without solid moral order. We begin with the children, all of whom are out of control. One is smoking; another is stealthily stealing a coin from a purse in the cupboard as a young man on the violin looks on smiling. Is he planning a heist as well? Will penury befall the family as the flattened, empty purses on view suggest? The toddler in a highchair looks down. Is he watching the pig which has pulled the spigot from the barrel, emptying it of its liquor, alluding to a Dutch saying that infers excessive drinking? Or is he plotting a reckless move that will send the pearl necklace in his hand crashing to the floor, strewing rolling pearls about the floor? Is that an account book on the floor? Uh oh – it's a sign of temporary wealth! The pig snuffling a rose recalls a proverb about waste. A woman, purportedly the mother, is out cold. Exhausted or inebriated? In any case, havoc reigns from lack of supervision. The dog eats from her dish – a Dutch metaphor for children shockingly ill-bred; a monkey (exotic pets signified wealth) toys with the clock that could refer to foolish waste of time. The duck roosted on the shoulder of a clergyman who reads lessons from scripture to an avid listener alludes to aimless chitchat. Featured in the center of the painting is a couple who display a familiarity that brings into mind the adage of the wages of sin. She, her legs apart, wears a fetching gown with alluring décolletage. The dangling pitcher she holds accounts for the glazed expression on her face, but neither distract from the coy manner in which she holds a glass of *vin rouge* suggestively close to the man's crotch. He brazenly has a leg draped over her knee, and smugly eyes another woman who ostensibly berates his behavior. Strewn about the floor are playing cards, a discarded hat, pretzels, a spilled tankard and more; people are gambling, drinking, wasting food – all of which denote carelessness. Hovering in a basket above the scene are crutches, a leper's clapper, what looks like a Damocles sword, switches for beating and other objects that are all ominous signs of woe to follow folly. (Folly too, wouldn't you think, to leave a fire in the background unattended). To drive the point home, Steen placed a slate on the bottom right (in Dutch) with the chalked dictum, "In good times, beware....," anticipating the comeuppance that inevitably results from dissolute behavior. Ah, but he gives the warning in such a beguiling and engaging way. A Dutch friend tells us that, to this day, a messy house is called a Jan Steen household! The household will be having a horrific headache the next morning, if the house doesn't burn down first.

Fig. 95. Steen. *Beware of Luxury.*

For extreme contrast, check out Pieter de Hooch's (1629-1683) *Woman and Child in a Pantry* (c. 1660) (Fig. 96). A loving exchange between a charming and smiling mother and small child, both neatly attired (the child is outfitted with walking ribbons), is portrayed in a spotless home. Even the checkered floors intimate a well ordered, traditional Dutch home, and their color lends warmth to the sparely furnished spaces. Details of order and careful moderation include a chair with carefully folded material on it, a pot that catches a potential drip from the barrel spigot and the small pitcher of liquid the mother hands the child. The scene and gesture are imbued with principles there are no idleness, waste or excess in this household, as compared with the chaos of Steen's work. A reference to solid familial unity is reflected with the simple inclusion of a portrait of a maternal figure in the room beyond. The open window alludes to God's light entering the home. Some view the image as an invitation for all to see and admire the home's exemplary Dutch values. The artist's composition enlarges the scene and, with geometric precision and light, complements the quiet beauty and joy of model home life.

Fig. 96. de Hooch. *Woman and Child in a Pantry.*

Adriaen van Nieulandt's (1587-1658) still life, *Kitchen Scene*, has the marks of a market more than an ordinary kitchen's interior. It might be interpreted à la Simon Shama (b. 1945) in *An Embarrassment of Riches* as a 17th century Netherlandish cornucopia of food as signs of prosperity and achievement. The still lifes reflected national pride and the wealth accumulated from enriching global trade. There always seemed for the ruling classes to be a surplus of food, and food itself was frequently celebrated in paintings, depicting exaggerated quantities of game and food of all varieties. A contrast here from the history of many other parts of Europe that experienced periods of famine from ergot epidemics, droughts, internecine wars and resurgent plague. Here, Nieulandt goes overboard in depicting *fruits de mer*, vegetables, breads, magnificent feathered birds and products of the hunt, inspiring the question, is this only a masterful still life? In the scene of freshly slaughtered animals and an excess of every kind of food is a well dressed buxom woman plucking a chicken taking heed of a greedy looking young man's instructions. In the background on the left, there is a small depiction of a biblical story that reveals the underlying moral intent of the artist, consistent with contemporaneous thinking that signs of temptations of the flesh and gluttony, of a surfeit of luxury, are emblematic of Dutch disdain for intemperance and here, a reminder of the transience of wealth and its bounty.

Fig. 97. van Nieulandt. *Kitchen Scene.*

Wealth in the Netherlands stirred vain desires for personal portraits to display in the home, and many commissioned artists for that purpose. The artists intuitively understood the unspoken aim: flatter the sitter, show the prosperity, but avoid ostentation. It was a challenge many artists brilliantly carried out. Bartolomeus van der Helst (1613-1670), born in Haarlem, moved to Amsterdam in 1636, where he quickly replaced Rembrandt as the favored portraitist. Until his death, he remained the leading painter of Amsterdam's patrician class. His work, in contrast to that of Rembrandt, radiated bright colors and were meticulously grand and polished in the tradition of the *fijnschilder* – the moniker given to fine detailed Dutch artists of the Golden Age. The portraits commonly displayed rich fabrics, imposing, even ceremonial stature and gestures, and, occasionally, subtle iconography. It's up to you to determine if the portrait of Gerard Andreisz Bicker (Fig. 98), painted by Bartolomeus van der Helst (1613-1670), is a sublime example of unabashed splendor or the poster child of an epidemic of obesity. Either way, there is no doubt about the painter's breathtaking skill. The young Gerard is resplendently garbed in red satin, intricate lace and silk gloves, clearly a pampered heir to the family fortune. His posture, if not the self-satisfied look directed towards the viewer, is complacent, haughty. The excess that contributed to this youngster's corpulence would not necessarily have been fodder for criticism in his time, for portliness indicated wealth and the means to indulge in an abundance of food. Van der Helst's skill in portraiture was such, had it been his intention, he could have chosen several modalities to make Gerard's dimensions less obvious. On the contrary, perhaps somewhat mischievously, he chose techniques that emphasize Gerard's bulk. The figure fills most of the frame, and the arms, positioned to reach the edge of the frame (and, in the instance of one arm, in fact goes beyond it), emphasize his size. Van del Helst exquisitely (take a gander at that velvet, that satin!) produced a magnificent portrait, faithfully recording the round facies of obesity, the door-handle chin, the dimpled fingers and general corpulence of the body. True to the explicit commissions to paint portraits that revealed class, wealth and opulence, there is no evidence van der Helst imbued his portrait of Gerard Andreisz Bicker with a subtle, yet elegant, moral message of the consequences of excess and the need for temperance, however the portrait, as has often been acknowledged, accentuates the profligate fortunes of the merchants of the time.

Fig. 98. van der Helst. *Gerard Bicker.*

The large and rich mercantile class of the 17th century commissioned an estimated 750,000 portraits. Calvinistic constraints were *de rigeur*, so that the background and any props that were inserted had to be modest, devoid of ostentatious display of wealth. Standing or full-length portraits reflected pride and therefore were assiduously eschewed.

Seventeenth century Dutch pride is manifested in the number of honorific paintings and colossal group portraits that used iconographic elements in basically three categories (medical, military and political) to identify individuals and their occupations* Individuals were always dressed in modest finery, held accoutrements suitably associated with their trade and generally were painted looking towards the viewer. Iconic examples are the *Anatomy Lesson of Dr. Tulp* (1.5 by 2.1 meters; five by seven feet.) and the *Night Watch* (3.7 by 4.3 meters; twelve by fourteen feet), both by Rembrandt van Rijn (1606-1669). The Dutch were proud of all their national accomplishments and eager to bequeath them to history; they defeated and expelled the Spanish who had conquered them, mastered the sea and the global trade it permitted, and celebrated their emergence as leaders in medical and scientific advances.

The many dissection honorifics produced throughout the Netherlands focused on the principals in portrait mode, rather than highlighting scientific or anatomical acumen. Nicholaes Tulp (1593-1674), the city anatomist of Amsterdam, is the most celebrated example, his fame ensured by Rembrandt's masterwork (Fig. 99). The painting depicts the public dissection of the thief Aris Kindt who was executed on January 16, 1632. Shown with his colleagues, Tulp is dissecting the left forearm of Kindt. Why public dissections? Physicians were eager to validate the nascent science of anatomy. Note the Caravaggisti elements in the painting – the sense of motion projected by several of the onlookers, the light streaming in from the left, the careful triangular composition that directs the eye to the dissection site. Dr. Tulp was portrayed outside of the dramatic framework and narrative in what amounts to a separate portrait of the esteemed anatomist.

---

*Honorifics were not a Dutch invention. *The Journey of the Magi to Bethlehem* by Benozzo Gozzoli (1420-1497), frescoes in the Medici Chapel, qualifies as an honorific painting, despite the religious reference since it glorifies Lorenzo de'Medici and family members and their retinue of powerful Florentines and allies from Milan. One can slip into the category Johan Zoffany (1733-1810), who also produced many honorifics, among them the *Royal Academy Class of 1772.*

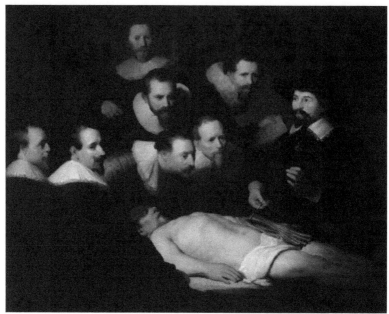
Fig. 99. Rembrandt. *The Anatomy Lesson.*

The mammoth sized *Night Watch* (Fig. 100) is considered Rembrandt's most famous work. It is a commissioned work of the militia chief Captain Frans Bannick (1605-1655) (he's the one wearing black with a bright red sash) in the company of his lieutenant van Ruytenburch (1600-1657), who is nattily dressed in golden yellow with a white sash (Yellow is said to have had an established association with victory). The glowing girl in gold to the left of the captain not only serves to compositionally highlight the hero of the piece, but has an emblematic purpose: the claws of the chicken that dangle from her belt represent the insignia of the arquebusiers. Likewise, the helmet of one of the members of the night watch who crosses in front of her holding a rifle is adorned with the company's emblem – the oak leaf. Rembrandt's treatment of his trademark chiaroscuro contrasted with brilliant light conducts the eye to the gallant principle subject who, with his lieutenant, strides forward. Energy, action and vigor swamp the painting, as the assembly appears to move forward as if they were the chorus in *Les Mis*. Look at that drummer to the right! Pride and delight palpable in his face as he stomps forward with a jubilant beat of the drum.

Fig. 100. Rembrandt. *The Night Watch.*

A unique type of portrait, the *tronie*, should be singled out. Always a face, *tronies* illustrate human physiognomy with various and always hyperbolic expressions. Often humorous, such the example shown here in Joos van Craesbeeck's (1625-1660) *Smoker* (Fig. 101), a man forever frozen in time with the expert strokes of paint brushes, he exhales smoke from his clay pipe. Despite disheveled hair and the insistently firm grasp of his bottle of schnapps, there is no narrative element to the work, a feature of *tronie* art that leaves interpretation to the imagination of a typically delighted viewer.

Rembrandt Harmenszoon van Rijn (1606-1669) was a prolific painter and print maker who depicted a multifaceted collection of portraits, self-portraits, genre, allegorical, mythological and biblical works. He never left the Netherlands, but was influenced by the Caravaggisti and the Flemish Baroque. Most appealing are his many self-portraits which reveal a pictorial biography of maturity and aging intimately and without vanity.

Fig. 101. van Craesbeeck. *The Smoker.*

In any museum around the world invariably there will be at least one Dutch painting of flowers from the Golden Age. Tulips were imported in the 16th century from the Ottoman Empire and the Netherlands today surely remains the land of the tulip. Dutch floral still lifes have rich symbolic meaning beyond emblems of wealth and creativity. They are glutted with harmonious images of elegant, compositionally spectacular, exquisitely balanced floral beauty. And more! Insects, butterflies, snails are often in the pictures, and not for purely decorative purposes. Many scholars have differing opinions and interpretations of the meanings of the iconography in these paintings, some of which overlap, but none of which are contradictory. Insects in paintings, for example, can reflect the idea that all of God's creations are important, or connote the pithy length of life there is for us all. We often see flies, beetles, dragonflies loitering on flowers and destructively nibbling away at them and their leaves. Butterflies signify both change (metamorphosis) and *vanitas*, i.e. the transient nature of life. Blemished or withered flowers also refer to the transience of life and eternal life. Check out Isaiah 40:8 – "The grass withers and the flowers fall, but the word of our God endures forever." It's interesting and enlightening to know that the flowers reflect God's creation and love, but in the here and now, the loveliness and appearance of freshness fill one with admiration as magnificent, beautiful to look at masterpieces. Rachel Ruysch's (1664-1750) *A Spray of Flowers* (Fig. 102), a compositionally perfect cluster of blossoms on a marble surface with two butterflies, a dragonfly and a beetle with its carapace open, ready to fly off as ants inch their way forwards, is an example. Still, it is important to know that the artist intended the painting to be a prudent – if lovely – reminder of the transience of life.

Fig. 102. Ruysch. *A Spray of Flowers.*

Other still life works flaunt the *fijnschilders'* technical expertise in masterful compositions that display exceptional artistic capability. Artful arrangements of crystalline wine glasses, polished silver bowls and pewter tankards with luminous reflections of light, meticulously painted comestibles, meats, nuts, cheeses and fruits, often with their peeled skins flaccidly dangling in graceful spirals from a clothed table whose fabric is visually established by the deft skill of the artist. The pictorially realistic depiction of such worldly, pleasure filled scenes in harmonious arrangements, typically have subtle iconographic moral nuance. Willem Claesz Heda (1594-1680) commands the field in this regard, and was renowned for his innovation of what was referred to as "breakfasts" or "banquets" still lifes. In the example shown here (Fig. 103), painted in muted colors, there are three glasses, one of which, a roemer by its shape, is half filled with wine. The meat pie is half eaten, a curled strip of lemon rind from the partially peeled lemon languidly hangs from the table, remnants of nuts are scattered about the tablecloth. Central to the scene is an upturned nautilus cup on a disheveled table with the table cloth shifted to one side of the table. Now to the meaning of it all. The exotic nautilus, with its intricate logarithmic spirals, collected from the far away Indo-Pacific Ocean by Dutch traders with other luxury items (tropical fruit, spices and sugar), represent the mathematical perfection in God's world of nature. The nautilus was a highly desirable collectible with a luxury price tag when crafted as a vessel banded with silver. The lemon is also an eatable treat reserved for the wealthy, as are nuts. But all good things come to an end. The pie is half-eaten. Although still delicious looking, it has lost its circular symmetry, and the lemon begins to show desiccation in the now stale post-feast scene. The fallen nautilus neatly corroborates the *vanitas* reminder of the ephemeral nature of all life – and luxury. The glass, therefore, is half empty!

Fig. 103. Claesz.Heda. *Still life with Nautilus cup.*

The sea was central and organic to Dutch life. It symbolized national identity through naval prowess and political independence, and, it came with the wealth accumulated through the global trade routes the Dutch established of spices, tropical foods, oriental porcelains and the exportation of fish, particularly the herring. By 1650, ninety-five percent of traffic across the North Sea into the Baltic was Dutch, its mercantile fleet nearly the size of the entire European fleet combined. The sea demanded great national stamina and effort in containing it with dikes and sea walls that necessitated constant vigilance and repair. Almost everywhere the Dutchman traveled, the sea was close by – coastal, inland bodies of water, canals and lakes that emerged from the saturated water tables of the countryside. The seascape or maritime landscape was ubiquitous in Netherlandish homes. Willem van de Velde II's (1633-1670) father was a marine painter who passed his skills on to his son. In *Dutch Man O'War and other Ships*, van de Velde depicts a proudly all Dutch scene. On a calm sea, every ship bears the colors of the Netherland, red white and blue streamers waving from the tops of masts. A perfectly blue sky with billowing clouds bespeaks a nation at peace, secure and confident. The harbor is full of ships that affirm the vast maritime power that was Holland. It is a proud painting that celebrates a national identity.

Fig. 104. van de Velde. *Dutch Man O'War and other Ships.*

Cityscapes were not in any way iconographic, but rather iconic reflections of Dutch civic pride, and were painted for just about every major city where they were proudly displayed in chamber halls and cities *stadhuizen*. Unusual for the times, but nevertheless the most famous of the genre is Jan Vermeer's (1632-1675) *View of Delft*, painted in 1660. We see the town from the south overlooking the River Schie. In the distance is the tower of the old church, resplendent in sunshine; the new church still in shadow, as dark clouds float out of the frame. The promise of a brilliant sunlight day is already apparent, however, in the overall luminous atmosphere of the painting, and, as the clock on the Schiedam gate informs, it is just after seven in the morning. There are town folk in the foreground, but still and quiet, complements to the stillness and tranquility that prevails. Vermeer's use of light and shadow in the sky and on the town's buildings, their reflections in the river, the crisp lines and controlled colors of this almost photographic painting combine to merit its rank as the most beautiful masterpiece cityscape of the Dutch Golden Age.

As a final note on Dutch paintings, let's have a look at artists' paintings of traditional Protestant churches. They usually painted the interiors in monochromic tones, with morning sunlight illuminating dark spaces.

Fig. 105. Vermeer. *View of Delft.*

The Netherlands was a marshland of the Rhine and Maas river deltas and over a third of the country was below sea level reclaimed by windmill pumps and dikes and contained by canals that laced the countryside. The environmental perspective therefore was such that the horizon was distant and low and the sky overwhelmed the field of vision. Thus, in city, sea and landscapes the skies consumed much of the painting.

111

The churches had imposing, yet simple, architectural elements. Long gone were statues, stained glass windows and altars. The visual focus was on the pulpit and the open bible on it. In the Calvinist tradition, churches were, in essence, meeting houses where worshipers gathered for edifying readings and sermons from scripture. The most prominent of artists of the genre were Pieter Saenredam (1597-1665) and Emanuel deWitte (1616-1691/1692). Portrayals of interiors depicted casual scenes in which graffiti is often seen on the base of large columns, unattended children and dogs roam about and people engage in conversation. Not uncommonly, a dog with a leg raised against a pillar was depicted, signifying that, in God's church, all natural things are acceptable. Emanuel de Witte (1617-1692) specialized in church interiors. His painting *Church interior, Amsterdam* (Fig. 106), embodies the genre. A dog lies behind a small group deep in conversation. A child with his toy, a stick-horse, holds a parent's hand. The artist shows a grave digger preparing an *ad sanctus* burial, casually chatting with an onlooker, appropriately just under a large commemorative plaque that has a *memento mori* skull on the top. The presence of God is manifest in the vertical proportions of the painting that has massive pillars that soar upward out of the frame into the heavens, for all we know. The figures are small – tiny – in contrast to the majesty of God. The interplay of light and shade contribute to the stately grandeur and serenity the picture defines.

Fig. 106. de Witte. *Church Interior Amsterdam.*

A final category to consider regarding Golden Age Dutch art is religious art. Images disappeared from churches under the new Protestant sects, but homes continued to commission works for private veneration. Usually the preference was for biblical motifs or New Testament themes about Christ. The Caravaggisti movement had reached the Netherlands in the early 17th century, and the influence of Caravaggio's religious paintings found their way into Dutch artistic expression. They were very popular with patrons.

Utrecht's Hendrick ter Brugghen (1588-1629) and Gerrit van Honthorst (1590-1656), studied art with the then mannerist painter Abraham Bloemart who had been influenced by the Italian movement in which grace and elegance were depicted in curious anatomical proportions – elongated limbs and necks, stylized facial features and poses and the like. Affected, even superficial, a strange artificiality often resulted. Ter Brugghen lived in Italy from 1604 to 1614, during which time he met Rubens and, most significantly, Caravaggio. Honthorst too lived in Italy and, like ter Brugghen, was bowled over by the phenomenal originality of Caravaggio's paintings. On their return to Utrecht, both artists applied the master's techniques to their own works. Bloemart and other Dutch artists observed, listened, learned and they too adopted the Caravaggisti style which spread throughout Europe. It is said Caravaggio was the most imitated artist in Western art. Rubens considered ter Brugghen's skill the greatest of all the Utrecht artists of his time. Most of ter Brugghen's paintings were daylight scenes similar in coloration and subject matter to Caravaggio's early works. In what is arguably his masterpiece, the strong influence of the mature Caravaggio is most evident: *St. Sebastian Tended by St. Irene* (Fig. 107) is a taut and intricate composition of three figures on different planes. Light streams into the painting from the left with a complex of arms reaching upwards, painted with lovely, controlled foreshortening. Shadow and light conjoin to present a drama of startling realism: a swollen hand from painful bindings; exhaustion on the face of the saint as death encroaches; bright light that draws attention to the boney and irregular physiognomy of St. Sebastian. The delicacy of expression and calm on the faces of the women who untie his hands and remove the arrows from his punctured body figure in the composition. The hands of the woman loosening the ties on the saint's hand frame the cyanotic extremity. The light brings St. Irene into view as a focal figure, and the white of her headpiece is repeated in the cloth entwined about St. Sebastian's body, a device that attracts the eye to St. Irene as she removes one of the arrows. The opulent gold and red cloth underneath St. Sebastian's body intimates his sanctity. The waning color of the sunlight in the sky to the right complements the mantle, another ruse to keep the eye on the principals. Disengaged from the viewer, the two women carry on with their distressing task in a suitably sparse, barren landscape as they release the broken body of the murdered saint.

Fig. 107. ter Brugghen. *St Sebastian tended by St. Irene.*

Honthorst's *Christ Before the High Priest* (Fig. 108) beautifully incorporates several of Caravaggio's techniques – a posed group of ordinary people dramatically enveloped in darkness and factitious light, and an air of mystery which, in this instance, suggests a tragic encounter. The high priest gestures toward the brightly lit figure of Christ who, with bound hands, resolutely awaits his adjudication. The muted and controlled half-tones of the canvas and the dual grouping of silent witnesses allow the vertical candle in the center of the painting to control the focus of the scene: on the one side, the high priest who sits in judgment, and, on the other, more illuminated and therefore more dominant, the figure of Christ.

Fig. 108. Honthorst's *Christ Before the High Priest*.

      The Utrecht Caravaggisti Honthorst and ter Brugghen bequeathed the style to prominent students such as Honthorst's student Peter Lastman (1583-1633), who went to Rome in 1604 to study Caravaggio's works. When back in Amsterdam in 1605, he instructed the techniques of Caravaggio to Rembrandt van Rijn (1606-1669), destined to be his most famous student. One glance at Rembrandt's *Simon's Song of Praise* or *The Presentation of Jesus in the Temple* (Fig. 109) plainly discloses the influence: mystical light from the left, a staged group, meaningful gestures artfully employed to highlight the principal characters, dramatic chiaroscuro.

Fig. 109. Rembrandt. *Simon's Song of Praise.*

Subtle influence of Dutch artists extended to just about every European country, most especially as social genre paintings. Roman countryside life was also popular in Italy, with a group of painters called the *Bamboccianti*, a colony of Dutch and Flemish artists active 1625-1700. In Venice, Pietro Longhi (1701-1785) produced elegant intimate interiors of mannered and staged groups of Venetians, each with their own story painted in light and shadow to great effect. Like Londoner William Hogarth (1697-1764), Longhi's works are a series of small moralistic "story-boards" that often comically unmask human foibles. His compatriot, Giovanni Canal (1697-1768), known as "Canaletto," found his muse in cityscapes with his grand, super-sized *verdute* of the waterways of Venice and social landscapes that incorporated Venetian waters with festive crowds and boatmen, all painted with meticulous, yet lively detail.

Genre paintings can be found as Spanish *bodegones* and *picaresques*, in French realist paintings, Victorian romantic scenes, German *biedermeier* and Japanese *ukiyo-e*. Whoa! Strike that last one, we said this was a Eurocentric look at iconography. There are so many beautiful art works worldwide, but we can't consider them all in one volume. Readers interested in a more global view will find the entire genre school on line; just keep in mind, it began with the Dutch.

Table five lists iconographs frequently used in these Dutch Golden Age paintings. It along with the other tables at the end of the book are intended as interpretative aids while our readers museum hop.

Our goal has been to expound on iconography, but scholars of Dutch painting are more exacting than we have been and they commonly use urban origins in their classification. They employ categories like "Leiden *fijnschilders*," "Haarlem School," "Delft style," or "Utrecht Caravaggisti." In analyzing the overall Dutch Golden age of painting and the public want of art, they note about two-thirds of homes had some piece of art, but that the art varied greatly both in quality and price. A small engraving could be purchased for about the price of a small fish, while a *fijnschilder,* like an opus of Gerrit Dou, could fetch 1,000 guilders or more, the cost of a comfortable Dutch house. They also note that there was a minority of Dutchmen who morally condemned art as being deceptive with respect to the real virtues and values of life, but that despite the scattered puritanical opposition, the populace embraced art as a unifying force that celebrated the nation and its accomplishments. Courtesy Jonathan Janson at *Essential Veermer*

Footnotes: Chapter Three.

1. Imported from Turkey, the cultivation of the tulip in the Netherlands began around 1590. They became the fourth leading export after gin, herring and cheese. By the Golden Age, the flower's popularity was such that bulbs were traded on the stock market and commanded higher and higher prices. Between 1636 to 1637, a period referred to as *tulipmania*, the price of bulbs skyrocketed. From November 12 to February 3 the price rose two hundred percent. At auction, bulbs could change hands several times a day, doubling in price with each transaction. Catastrophically in human and economic terms, the plague flared up on February 4, killing lives and financial trade in Haarlem. In any case, there and elsewhere buyers had reached their bidding limits. Prices had reached too high a level, and speculators who bought bulbs for a quick and profitable flip found no buyers. The market collapsed, and, by May 1st, prices were back to November 12 levels, and many a fortune had been lost. The tulips endured.

Calvin: As my artist's statement explains, my work is utterly incomprehensible and is therefore full of deep significance.

Bill Watterson, *Calvin and Hobbes*

Chapter Four: A Class of Their Own - Iconographic Erratics

In art and its iconographic landscape, there are works that stretch the boundaries of art classification we have termed "Iconographic Erratics."* The term neatly serves our purpose to discuss a number of art works that are far beyond traditional categories – isolated pieces removed from traditional art classifications. *History paintings* incorporate mythological works, allegory, religious themes and battle scenes. G*enre paintings* explore ordinary representations of everyday – and especially domestic – life. *Landscape paintings* focus on natural scenery, and, perhaps as a sub-heading, include maritime or seascapes, cityscapes, gardens, and even interiors. *Still life paintings* show anything that is not moving. *Portrait paintings* depict individuals and groups, as self-portraits, full-faced, in profile, sitting, standing, on horseback, etc. Iconographic erratics supply a format in which to discuss unique works that do not quite fit into any art categories.

Fig. 110.   Glacial erratic in Yosemite Park.

*A word purloined from references to geological oddities formed by glaciers that sculpted and abraded the earth, plucking up colossal boulders and carrying them along as its massive weighted ice snaked across the terrain. Receded glaciers left behind these erratics deposited in an entirely different geological setting (Fig. 110).

To exemplify the point, *La Gioconda,* despite the mystique that has evolved regarding that inscrutable smile, does not make the cut as an erratic. It rightly belongs in the ranks of portraits, and a brilliant and original one at that. Pity the "Mona Lisa" has been reduced to a cliché, a subject for pop art and cheap music and a painting gawked at by millions of tourists just off the bus who only take time to snap a photo, sadly missing the opportunity to recognize the portrait was a stunning departure from the tradition of the times.[1]

With regards to what we have classified as erratics, look at the back cover of this book for illustrations of two iconographs. Millennia old, they have endured into modern times, but no longer have genuine emblematic depth. In centuries past, even from ancient times, somatic symbols, now clear as dish water as is iconography, are displayed in museums and even on architectural ruins. The relief of a penis is Roman, first century CE. The inscription, *hic habitats Felicitas* identifies it as a good luck charm. It could refer to fertility, productivity, wealth or monetary fortune. It invoked the goddess Felicitas, not Fortuna, for the latter was unpredictable and capable of inflicting bad luck. In contrast, Felicitas always invoked her divine power in a positive manner. The sculptural *Sheela na gig* is unusual in that the emblem was more commonly depicted in relief. Figurative carvings of naked hags such as the *Sheela* always had an exaggerated vulva which they splayed open with their hands, symbols commonly worked into the stonework of a church, monastery or castle. Found in Ireland and England, they were always grotesque and intended to ward off evil or bad fortune, although some scholars suggest they were intended to caution monks from women and their evil ways. Do these objects qualify as art? Well, Greek and Roman body part *exvotos* (breasts, uteruses, bowels, legs, eyes, ears, arms, etc.) and tombstones are now standard inventory in art museums, so why not include here a carved stone penis and vulva as examples of art erratics? *

*Actually, the D'Orsay reinforces our assertion. We won't reproduce it here but check out Wikipedia for *L'origine du monde* (1866) painted by Gustave Courbet (1819-1877) for the erotic cabinet of an Ottoman diplomat. It's quite an eye-opener.

Mystical-Erratic.
There are several mystical works relevant to this subheading, among them some of the fantastical fantasies by Hieronymus Bosch (c. 1450-1516), the prophetic drawings and paintings of William Blake (1757-1827) and Mattias Grünewald's (1470-1528) *The Temptation of St. Anthony.* In 1514, Albrecht Dürer (1471-1528) engraved an enigmatic allegorical image, entitled *Melencholia 1* (Fig. 111). The engraving bears no reference to the melancholia of the Hippocratic and Galenic "Four humors" (*Choler, Phlegma, Sanguine, Melancholia*) as the primary elements that comprise human temperaments. Critics suggest Dürer's frame of reference is to the first of Agrippa's classification of Melancholy's qualities: *Melencholia Imaginativa,* i.e. artistic creativity, a Renaissance assumption for artistic geniuses. The engraving reflects Dürer's dissatisfaction with his artistic endeavors. It is obvious the wreathed Delphic winged figure in the disordered scene of iconographic pay dirt is miserable. She sits dark and skulking, her expression otherwise vapid, presumably devoid of creative inspiration. She holds a caliper in her hand. The scene is cluttered with inert geometric forms and building tools, code for mathematical precision and achievement, and a reference to Dürer's application of mathematical equations he applied to his artwork. Chaotically scattered about are unused measuring and building tools – a plumb line, weight, a plane, hammer and nails – all references to intellectual vigor in the Renaissance world. In this instance, the artist suggests the lack thereof. A magic numerology square in which the numbers add up to 34 regardless of how they are totaled, has, on the bottom line in the center, 1514, the year Durer engraved the work and, poignantly, the year Dürer's mother died. Was it a year in which his creative juices withered? There's a spiritual as well as creative crisis going on, as seen in the *memento mori* of a faintly visible skull on the surface of a massive geometric rhombohedron, the hourglass with sand, signifying time running out, and a mute bell that, when ringing, announces a death. A scale, emblematic of weighing spiritual matters, is empty and balanced, suggesting loss of ideation. A dejected putto (who represents knowledge), sits on a millstone poised to write on a wax tablet; by his expression, he has writer's block. A sleeping dog – usually a symbol of loyalty – is cachexic, symbolic of starved senses. The comet flashing across the sky evokes its association with Saturn. Countless studies of the work have attempted to demystify its meaning, and heaven knows, these writers don't presume to one up any experts by suggesting a definitive interpretation. In all, it can be asked what is wrong with the central figure? Does she represent a goddess of inspiration who is baffled, for whom there are no creative impulses, an errant muse without an idea?" Perhaps, it's all simply, as art historian Erwin Panofsky suggested, Dürer with all passion spent. The influence of Durer's engraving of *Melencholia* extended all over the European continent and lasted for more

than three centuries.   It was the first time the Renaissance concept of melancholy transmuted from the plane of scientific and pseudo-scientific folklore to the higher echelon of art. Whichever way you choose to interpret this work, it is a magnificent *Meisterstiche* – master engraving – rich in texture and shadowing with extraordinary three-dimensionality and an enthralling, enigmatic and complex storyline crammed with iconographical references.

Fig. 111. Dürer. *Melencholia 1.*

The Ages of Man: The allegory of the Ages of Man describes man's inexorable passage through life from birth to death. It is a sobering theme, full of emotive proportions that address the human condition. The singularly Western motif has no parallel in the Eastern world, and its concepts, with ancient roots, have been fundamentally unchanged through millennia. It can easily be discussed as belonging to the realm of death iconography (which has been done) but sometimes posits conundrums regarding where to apply the theme in the categories of art symbolism. Because The Ages of Man refers to all the cycles of life's wonders, with William Shakespeare (1564-1616) the inspirational muse,* we have dubbed it an erratic.

*All the world's a stage,

And all the men and women merely players;
They have their exits and their entrances;
And one man in his time plays many parts,
His acts being seven ages. At first the infant,
Mewling and puking in the nurse's arms;
And then the whining school-boy, with his satchel
And shining morning face, creeping like snail
Unwillingly to school. And then the lover,
Sighing like furnace, with a woeful ballad
Made to his mistress' eyebrow. Then a soldier,
Full of strange oaths, and bearded like the pard,
Jealous in honor, sudden and quick in quarrel,
Seeking the bubble reputation
Even in the cannon's mouth. And then the justice,
In fair round belly with good capon lin'd,
With eyes severe and beard of formal cut,
Full of wise saws and modern instances;
And so he plays his part. The sixth age shifts
Into the lean and slipper'd pantaloon,
With spectacles on nose and pouch on side;
His youthful hose, well sav'd, a world too wide
For his shrunk shank; and his big manly voice,
Turning again toward childish treble, pipes
And whistles in his sound. Last scene of all,
That ends this strange eventful history,
Is second childishness and mere oblivion;
Sans teeth, sans eyes, sans taste, sans everything.

As You Like It, Act II, Scene VII

The Pythagoreans (c. 500 BCE), whose philosophy and ideas regarding man's relationship to nature followed nature's cycles, categorized the Ages of Man into four stages: infancy, childhood, maturity and old age. To each age a season was ascribed. Spring represented infancy; summer, man's childhood; autumn spotlighted man in his mature years, and winter, nature's season of dormancy, ushered in man's decline, old age and death. To the early medieval mind, the Ages of Man was a pagan description of man's physical progression in life. It remained a secular and pagan concept in the newly Christianized West until patristic scholars adopted it to explain man's place in nature within the context of Christian exegesis that adjusted the ages to the Hippocratic hebdomad or the *septimum* of *infantia, puer, adolescens, iuvenis, vir, senior* and *senex*. Early depictions of the Seven Ages of Man commonly featured in the "Wheel of Fortune" in Fortuna's grasp was a moralistic device intended to illustrate life's brevity as seen in *Moralia super Bibliam* by Niccolo de Lyra (c. 1450) (Fig. 112).

Fig. 112. *Moralia super Bibliam*

Fig. 113. Grien. *The Ages of Man.*

Hans Baldung Grien (c.1484-1545) departed from both the tetrad and hebdomad model and used three figures in his *Ages of Man* (Fig. 113), an early Renaissance painting (c. 1485) imbued with a gloomy Gothic moral lesson. The infant is incidental to the painting's focus on the startling contrast of an exquisite Venus-like young woman transformed with age into a withered hag. A grisly figure of death holds an hourglass that symbolizes the sands of time that constantly ebb, and the broken staff is symbolic of the end of life. The painting's *memento mori* iconography could hardly be more explicit. The glass globe on top of the hourglass represents the fragility of life. The owl is a harbinger of death and the barren landscape's tree and stump reinforce the aura of death from which no one can escape. (We'll visit this image again in the last chapter). Tiziano's *The Ages of Man* (Fig. 114) depicts *Infantia* as two cherubic babes as Cupid watches them in sleep, *Iuvenis* as a lovely woman, amorously holding flutes (an echo of the Bard: "If music be the food of love...."), *Vir*, a nude in a Giorgionesque world, and *Senex* (who resembles St. Jerome in the wilderness) who contemplates, not one but two skulls, the definitive iconoclass of death. The thematic Ages of Man was very popular, and every museum has some version of it. The motif always served to admonish, "To everything there is a season, and a time to every purpose under the heaven. A time to be born and a time to die...." (*Ecclesiastes* 3:1-2).

Fig. 114. Titian. *The Ages of Man*.

In the *Stanza della Segnatura* of the Vatican, the stunning frescos on the four walls, tondos by Raphael Sanzio (1483-1520), are considered the artist's masterpiece. Each section represents a distinct branch of knowledge. In the philosophy group of what has come to be known as *The School of Athens*, due homage is given by this Renaissance giant to the rediscovered classical world and the geniuses whose works and reputations endure to the present day. The groups to which they have been ascribed by scholars facilitate a study of the work. Plato and Aristotle imperially stand center stage flanked by their apostles. In the right foreground Astronomy is represented by Strabo and Ptolemy who stands next to Euclid and his students of mathematics. Pythagoras, philosopher and mathematician, is shown with a musician, a reference to his work on music theory. Hypatia (350-415), the great Alexandrine mathematician, dressed in white, stands

126

behind the Pythagoras group. Socrates with his cup and Diogenes are there. To our interest as it relates to the subject of the Ages of Man, is the Epicurus group.

Fig. 115. Raphael. *The School of Athens* (detail).

Raphael exhibited a playful inclination in his great work: he painted the faces of people he knew to represent philosophic figures. He also, in our view, indisputably included the theme of the Ages of Man in the lower left corner of the painting that celebrates the great sages of the Western world – where Epicurus (341-270 BCE) stands at the base of a column pleasurably engrossed in a book. Corpulent, he is wearing a wreath of fig leaves emblematic of the hedonism associated with Epicureans. Epicurus rejected the idea of an afterlife and posited the aim of life was to be happy and to seek pleasure. Raphael ingeniously refuted his philosophy with a virtually universally accepted belief in an afterlife and the imperative to prepare for it with a statement of his own: he used Ovid's definition of the Four Ages of Man as a *memento mori*, in a group that surrounds Epicurus. The child, *puer* props up his book, a handsome youth, *iuvenis* stands behind his left shoulder, the grown man with both hands on Epicurus' shoulders is *vir* and the bearded man is *senex** As an Ages of Man motif, figures of the child, youth and young and old man clarify their presence in a work that extols Greek philosophic thought and highlights the irony of juxtaposing them next to a hedonist.

*The identity of the man remains contested as either the pre-Socratic philosopher Zeno or the image of Metrodorus of Lampsacus, a friend of Epicurus.

Social Politic: In 1533, Hans Holbein the younger (c. 1497-1543) painted *The Ambassadors*. Two men stand before a curious double tiered table. On the left is Jean de Dinteville, French ambassador to Henry VIII's court and Roman Catholic. On the right is Georges de Selva, a French Roman Catholic bishop and diplomat with close ties to Rome. There are an inexhaustible number of items in the painting open to political, religious and moral interpretation. On the upper table tier are several scientific instruments related to the cosmos imbued with emblematic meaning, including a celestial globe, quadrant, torquetum (to measure celestial coordinates) and a cylindrical sundial that of all things, establishes the date of the painting – Good Friday, 11 April, 1533. On the lower tier are worldly items: a globe, a mathematics book, a lute with a broken string and an open hymnal; all seemingly straightforward, until one assesses the political and religious tumult that occurred in England in that year. The instrument with a broken string represents discord and is strategically placed next to a Lutheran hymnal. The math book is open to "division" or *dividirt*. Holbein himself had been caught up in the tumultuously divisive issues of Reformation Europe (and managed to straddle the fence, having been both sympathetic to Roman Catholic Erasmus's principles and to Thomas More, martyr. (Holbein ultimately became King Henry VIII's court painter and a follower of reformist philosophy). Levitating before the figures is an extraordinary, disproportionate, over the top anamorphic skull, appreciated as such only from a precise angle to the right. The painting surely was intended to hang in a stairwell where anyone ascending the steps would be jolted, scared witless at the sight of the huge, quintessential *vanitas* symbol. De Dinteville's hat, interestingly, has a medallion with a tiny skull on it. In the far upper left of the painting, a crucifix is somewhat hidden, a compositional counterpart to the *memento mori* skull.   The two diplomats (who are known to have been friends) are separated, one dressed in elaborate secular splendor and the other in rich clerical garb. There is apparently no inference of theological differences between them, and presumably both would have supported Rome's traditional rather than Henry's radical positions.   In 1533, sixteen years had passed since Luther's seismic break from the Roman Church, and, in England that year, Henry VIII married Ann Boleyn in January, Cranmer – the Archbishop of Canterbury – in May declared Henry's marriage to Catherine of Aragon invalid and sanctioned Henry's marriage to Boleyn. The two diplomats would have been caught in the middle of that political and religious maelstrom. What would have been Holbein's view? In addition to showing off his artistic skills by an amalgam of portraiture, still life, anamorphosis and *memento mori*, Holbein appears to have made a powerful statement regarding the incidental importance of worldly matters in comparison with the inevitable end to life and judgment of our lives that awaits us in heaven. A comprehensive and well worth reading analysis of this outstanding, enigmatic painting was written by John North.[2]

Fig. 116. Holbein. *The Ambassadors.*

William Hogarth (1697-1764) and Jean Geoffroy (1853-1924) both produced social-political paintings, diametric opposite observations of their contemporary commonweal and public health. The iconography of each is unique and intended to convey important social messages in dramatically divergent contexts.

During the first half of the 18th century, Great Britain imposed a duty on imported spirits, but allowed the distillation of gin without tax. The result was a socially dysfunctional intemperate period labeled the "Gin Craze." The consumption of gin increased logarithmically, forcing Parliament to pass several Gin Acts in hopes of stemming excessive drinking related to the cheaply attainable alcohol and the consequent daily inebriation and widespread debauchery among the populations' lower ranks. By mid-century, ten liters of gin per person per year was being swilled. An anti-gin campaign was launched, and clergymen, writers and artists joined the effort. Hogarth's iconic engraving, *Gin Lane* (1751) (Fig. 117) savagely illustrated the social ills caused by alcoholism. On the left, a ragged woman, desperate for gin money, attempts to pawn her pots and pans; next to her, a carpenter offers his trade tool, a saw, for sale. A desperately hungry beggar stands in

129

the foreground besides a man and a dog who gnaw at a bone in tandem. The city scene in the background depicts a derelict building, a disintegrating building and a society in which the dead are coffined in the streets, a man hangs himself in the rafters, a baby is impaled by a madman who strikes himself on the head with a bellows and those inebriated beyond walking are carted about in a wheelbarrow. On the far right, a woman sedates her infant with either Godfrey's cordial (opium mixed with treacle), a popular opiate, or perhaps even gin. It is the central figure that most scandalizes and wrests a shiver of abhorrence. Hogarth ominously placed the cachectic figure of impending death at the woman's feet in the lower right corner of the painting. The woman is a mother reduced to prostitution (note the syphilitic sores on her legs), who, overtaken in a drunken stupor, her hand limp in a snuff box, is pitifully oblivious to the fatal tumble of her nursing child into the alley, wherein is located the entrance to the *Gin Royal* Pub per the caption on the establishment's tankard that marks the site. Inscribed on the pub's threshold is "Drunk for a penny, dead drunk for twopence, clean straw for nothing." The pendant to this work, another of Hogarth's social commentaries, is *Beer Street*. The consumption of beer was encouraged to dissuade people from drinking gin, but beer, as Hogarth sardonically observed, was equally inebriating and produced the same degree of debauchery and mayhem.

Fig. 117. Hogarth. *Gin Lane.*

Fig. 118. Geoffroy. *La Goutte de Lait de Belleville.*

What a happy relief to contrast *Gin Lane* with its categorical converse, Geoffroy's *La Goutte de Lait de Belleville*, (The drop of milk of Belleville) (Fig. 118), an idealized portrait of the nineteenth century French *puériculture* social welfare system that was dedicated to the well-being of children. The scene is a pediatric clinic where babies are being examined to measure issues of growth, development and nutrition. Two central figures draw us in: the nursing mother in the foreground consulting with physicians, and a mother who stands behind her showing off her baby even as she proudly admires her chubby, healthy infant in arms. An apparent older sister who stands next to the mother placidly plays second fiddle. The room is packed with beaming, nurturing and adoring mothers and beautiful, thriving infants and children with a support team of caring physicians. Absent the halos, these are no madonnas or saints, but admirable exemplars of motherhood and the salubrious effects good parenting and pediatric care have on children.

War and Politics: Francisco Goya (1746-1828) was no stranger to madness, despite the many fine and handsome portraits with which he earned his keep. Several of his works bear marks of witchcraft, ghosts, gremlins, horror and abject depravity. His *Caprichos* belong to a subset genre that will be reviewed, but one of his most iconic paintings, the colossal (2.7 by 3.4

meters; 9 by 11 feet.) *El Tres de Mayo*, belongs to no genre, and here is designated an erratic. The back story is the subjugation of Spain by Napoleon in 1808 and the brutal treatment of its citizens. It was painted years after the horrific political drama that took place on the third of May, 1808, when French soldiers systematically executed Spanish citizens. Goya's bold denunciation of the event is brilliantly testified to in the terrified and despairing faces of the innocent victims and their emotionally detached, faceless assassins he painted. Absorbing the power of the painting, an image in our minds is generated of a modern Goya tackling a painting of an isolated, anonymous and safe pilot 10,000 miles away in a remote, emotionally void control room who pushes a button that sends a drone to kill, invariably and predictably, so called collateral damage of blameless unseen victims. *El Tres de Mayo* was but a prelude to the slaughter of the guiltless of the past two hundred years in which civilians, not combatants, became the principal casualties of senseless wars.

Fig. 119. Goya. *El Tres de Mayo.*

A very different purpose is reflected in another French conflict in a monumental (2.7 by 3.4 meters; 9 by 11 feet) painting by Eugène Delacroix (1798-1863) entitled *La Liberté Guidant le Peuple* (Liberty leading the people) (Fig. 120). The entire composition is charged with patriotic energy of the fierce three days of political fighting in 1830 against the Bourbon King Charles X that ultimately forced him to abdicate. It resembles a commemorative battle work, but its narrative was created for political purposes, and as such, it is in our view an erratic – on the grand scale. An allegory calculated to acclaim the collective heroes of the revolt, Lady Liberty, semi-nude, is a classical goddess figure wearing the Phrygian cap of liberty and is barefoot like the sans-culottes of the Revolution of 1789. In her right hand, brandishing the *tricolore* flag of the Revolution, she spurs on an avalanche of insurgents over the barricades. In her left hand, she carries a bayoneted musket, marching over the dead and dying of both *citoyens* and *militaires du roi*. She is surrounded by Parisian citizen soldiers with a sea of swords and bayonets who storm forwards in the rising smoke of the uprising. There is a street urchin wielding pistols, a *prolétaire* with a cutlass and a top-hatted dandy.* In the background haze, the towers of Notre Dame can be seen. The romantic composition is formed triangularly by Liberty, who is flanked by a whitish plume of smoke and the citizens following her. Placed off center, the figure creates an asymmetry that directs focus to the people she is encouraging to advance. Chromatically, the scattered blues and reds enhance attention to the tricolor banner fluttering in the wind.

Fig. 120. Delacroix. *La Liberté Guidant le Peuple.*

*Delacroix was present at the barricades during those three fateful days. He personally knew the 12 year old boy. The dandy is a self-portrait.

133

There is yet another example of a war and politics erratic (suggesting all these paintings could be nascent examples of a genre of their own). All mandate huge canvasses. All have a political and social statement. In 1936, Pablo Picasso (1881-1973) had accepted a commission for an artwork to exhibit in the Spanish Pavilion at the 1937 Paris World's Fair. On 26 April, 1937, Picasso had his theme. He painted the more than 3.4 by 7.6 meter (11 by 25 feet) *Guernica* (Fig. 121) in outraged response to the nefarious aerial attack on this small village of no military strategic value by German and Italian bombers aiding fascist General Francisco Franco's army. For maximum ruin and deaths, planes bombarded the city center on a market day for three hours, dropping 31 tons of explosives and incendiary bombs at low altitude and strafing mostly women and children with machine guns as they tried to flee. It was the first terror aerial bombing in history, a cold blooded calculated tactic to terrorize anti-Franco citizens. The news shocked the world as it had Picasso. The painting has been termed a narrative abstraction, but narrative alone suffices as a descriptive classification. It has a stunning impact (especially when viewed for the first time), with mammoth sized images of suffering, death, destruction, violence and chaos.   Fittingly considered the greatest anti-war painting of all times, the monochrome bleakness of grey, white and black intensify the heartbreak of the images: a wide-eyed bull seems paralyzed by fear. The image of a woman in grief as she cradles her dead child is heartrending. A horse screams in agony, seemingly disemboweled. A dismembered soldier lies dead, still grasping his sword with an open wound, like the stigmata of Christ, visible on his hand. Daggers simulate the screams being emitted everywhere; a woman's terrorized screams can almost be heard as her head and arms reach out of a window. On the right, a woman, her arms thrust upwards, is being devoured by flames. All is chaos, madness. *Guernica,* a unique and provocative work defies categorization. It has come to powerfully represent the cruelty, evil and horror of war.[3]

Fig. 121. Picasso. *Guernica.*

Psychological: Goya's *Los Caprichos*, is a series of 80 prints of aquatint etchings produced between 1797 and 1798. They depict what he called "...the foibles and follies...in any civilized society [of] prejudices, deceitful practices which custom, ignorance or self-interest have made usual." The prints are scathing in their depiction of Spanish high society: how they treated the poor, the sick, the homeless and peasants. We offer just two examples. Number 3 is titled "*Que viene el Coco*" (the boogeyman comes) (Fig. 122). Two terrified children seek solace and safety in their mother's arms, while she enigmatically stares at *el Coco*. On the surface it is a scolding of parents who threaten their children with the boogeyman, but is it possible the intention was to depict a mother looking upon death? Number 43, "*El Sueño de la Razón produce Monstros*" (Fig.123). The "Sleep of reason produces monsters," makes better sense when the full epigram is read: "Imagination abandoned by reason produces impossible monsters; united with her, she is the mother of the arts and source of their wonders." The etching shows a man sleeping, his head and arms on his drawing desk, with numerous owls and bats suspended around him, associations in Spanish folk lore of mystery and evil. Goya expresses the nightmare of the artist, who in his sleep loses psychic controls that mitigate ignorance and folly. All the *caprichos* are psychologically intense, hellish, and often terrifying.

Fig. 122. Goya. *Que Viene el Coco.*

Fig. 123. Goya. *El Seuño de la Razón produce Monstros.*

Edvard Munch (1863-1944) painted four versions of the spectacular erratic, *The Scream* (Fig. 124). An agonized, androgynous figure races towards the viewer, crazed, in psychic, not somatic, pain. With hands on the ears, the distorted skull-like head seemingly is about to explode. A swirl of psychedelic color* of the background water seamlessly extends into the sky at what seems to be sunset, reinforcing the surrealistic aura, relieved only by two figures on the bridge who stand inertly in the background. By Munch's own admission, the painting is largely autobiographical. "One evening I was walking along a path, the city was on one side and the fjord below. I felt tired and ill. I stopped and looked out over the fjord - the sun was setting, and the clouds turned blood red. I sensed a scream passing through nature.... It seemed to me that I heard the scream. I painted this picture, painted the clouds as actual blood. The color shrieked."[4] Interestingly, the original German title Munch gave the painting was *"The Scream of Nature.* Anyone who doesn't think this psychological drama sends shivers up one's spine should have his head examined.

---

*Norwegian meteorologist Helene Muri speculates that Munch may have witnessed an atmospheric phenomenon known as nacreous clouds which are iridescent and form during the winter in northerly latitudes. Smithsonian.com. April 26, 2017.

Fig. 124. Munch. *The Scream.*

The following two erratics present a challenge to describe, beyond commenting they are brilliant, beautiful and bizarre. At first sight mythological, they do not have any established mythological reference. Giorgio Barbarelli da Castelfranco (1477-1510), a Venetian, painted *The Tempest* (Fig. 125) around 1508. The storm brewing in the sky over the cityscape on the upper part of the canvas is completely divorced from the lower landscape of stream and countryside. A bridge, in fact, separates the two. In the countryside, a soldier stands to the left, and a woman is breast feeding on the right. Each seems unaware of the other's presence. His glance, although in her direction, appears to bypass her altogether. She looks enigmatically at the viewer without purpose or emotion. It helps to know that, Giorgione's work is esteemed because of his technical skill and beautiful compositions but is renowned mostly for the mysterious uncertainty of the meaning of his paintings. Its fame assuredly will endure as the first landscape in Western art, if nothing else.

Fig. 125. Giorgione. *The Tempest.*

What *was* Édouard Manet (1832-1883) thinking? That might be the thought that comes to mind when first seeing *Le Déjeuner sur l'herbe* (The Luncheon on the Grass) (Fig. 126). The painting was rejected by the prestigious Salon that year, and Manet exhibited it as *Le Bain* (The Bath) at the *Salon des Refusés*, where it was purportedly the biggest attraction, generating laughter, derision and scandal. In the background is a scantily dressed woman, bathing. In the foreground there is a nude woman sitting casually, almost coquettishly, looking past the viewer. Two smartly suited men sit between them, incomprehensibly engaged in conversation with each other, oblivious to the nude's voluptuous presence. The *raison d'être* for the title, remnants of their luncheon, rests at the base of the painting on the left. It wasn't the first painting to depict nudes with clothed counterparts (see Titian's *Concert Champêtre*), and supposedly Manet had Titian in mind when he painted *Le Déjeuner sur l'herbe*. It caused quite a stir in its time. With its stark contrast between a sylvan scene and the seemingly superimposed figures, it is said to be a departure point from the old to the new and modern. A logical interpretation of this lovely, if puzzling, masterpiece has yet to be proposed. We are still looking for one.

Fig. 126. Manet. *The Luncheon on the Grass.*

Homage to a master. John Singer Sargent (18561925) had Velasquez's masterpiece, *Las Meninas* in mind when, in 1882, he painted the square 2.1 meter (7 feet) masterpiece of his own, *The Daughters of Edward D. Boit* (Fig. 127). Four sisters all wear identical pinafores, the attire of childhood, but each project separate personas. All are emotionally and physically detached and disengaged from each other and us, although the youngest, sitting on the floor, having been distracted from child play with her doll, looks passively at the viewer. Her older sister stands to the left. She also is looking forwards, but without emotion. In the threshold, between large blue oriental vases, half-enveloped in darkness, stand the two older children. The girl on the right stares blankly at the observer. The oldest sister sullenly leans against a vase, her face and eyes in shadow tilted downwards, her posture a classic of adolescent aloofness. The background chiaroscuro is mysterious, as are the figures of all the children. It is as if Sargent is considering their passage into an unknown reality of an adult world and a concomitant loss of youthful innocence. Sargent's composition violates, but to great effect, a basic premise of portraiture in favor of exploring the emotive differences of childhood's stages of growing up. The unusual placement of the subjects alone deviates from the conventions of portraiture, and the artist explores, as did Velasquez in his masterpiece, a rich and provocative psychological study.

Fig. 127. Sargent. *The Daughters of Henry Boit.**

*Another Sargent masterpiece is a war erratic infused with intense psychological anguish. In *Gassed* (1919), an immense WWI scene after a battle the artist witnessed projects an archetype of the staggering crime against humanity that is war. In the foreground above a harrowing 'border' of suffering – soldiers in agony strewn across the landscape – ten men rendered sightless from searing mustard gas, eyes covered in bandages, linked together by their hands, unsteadily move forward, guided by an orderly whose movements suggests it is a routine mission. One afflicted soldier turns to vomit; another timorously lifts one leg in a pitiful effort to step forward. This disturbing image enables the viewer to grasp the future lives of these mentally and spiritually broken, shell shocked human wreckage destined to cope, perhaps for life, with post-traumatic stress syndrome. Imperial War Museum, London. GAP ygEoPGLZRQzeg. WC.

Footnotes: Chapter Four

1. Unique, *La Gioconda*, is unlike any portrait of the period. The serene and handsome woman looks directly at her admirers in a pleasingly natural and lifelike manner. Moreover, distinct from other portraits in Leonardo's world that mostly focused on the face and upper torso, he painted her almost full figure to the waist, with her hands comfortably at rest on an armchair. Leonardo da Vinci (1452-1519) introduced a technique called *sfumato* to produce gradual modulation of tone and color, notable in his subject's face, further softening its expression (and thereby emphasizing that seemingly tantalizing smile.) The background is another of da Vinci's innovations. What is that lovely creature before us doing in the middle of a vast and vague landscape that goes on into infinity? Well, it provides quite a contrast, and enhances the power of portrait by placing the subject in a realm beyond ordinary reality into a world of the imagination where she continues to enchant and confound us. Da Vinci scholar Kenneth Kelle intriguingly attributes *La Gioconda's* contented smile to pregnancy. Note the position of her hands, the puffiness under the eyes and of the fingers, and the drape of clothing to obscure an enlarged abdomen. (Kelle, 1983).

2. North, John. *The Ambassador's Secret: Holbein and the World of the Renaissance*. London: Bloombsbury Acadmic, 2005.

3. An anecdote tells of a German officer who saw a photograph of the *Guernica* in Picasso's Paris apartment and asked, "Did you do this?" to which Picasso responded, "No, you did."

4. Hughes, Robert. *The Spectacle of Skill.* NY: Knopf, 2015. P. 342

Art comes to you proposing frankly to give nothing but the highest quality to your moments as they pass.

Walter Pater (1839-1894) in History of the Renaissance

Chapter Five: A Matter of Life and Death

Death – the inevitable end to which we all are subjected – is difficult to come to terms with, and most of us avoid discussing it. George Elliot referred to people having 'joined the invisible choir,' an entry, surely in the dictionary of euphemisms that exists to make the unthinkable bearable: someone passed on, or over, or, recently, just passed. One hears she went to her maker, as if there was a body shop for reconstruction. You know them: he went home, perished, is at peace, or is at rest. That's for sure, eternal peace and rest. It can all be so unsettling. Sometimes superstitions surface: His number came up, or, it was his destiny and, when it's your time, it's your time. Sometimes, being flip, dysphemisms take the edge off the dismay: so and so croaked, is pushing up the daisies, bitten the dust, checked out, fizzled out, cashed in his chips, kicked the bucket,* went west, bought the farm, gave up the ghost (even the French use that one – *rendre l'âme.*) Our preference cites the Bard. In Shakespeare's Hamlet, Act I, scene 2, Gertrude says to her son, "Thou knows't 'tis common, all that lives must die/ Passing through nature to eternity." Hamlet tells her, "Ay, Madam, 'tis common," and Gertrude retorts, "If it be so, why seems it so particular with thee?" Why, indeed. Genuinely distressed or irreverently dismissive, the end result is the same: reminders of our common fate cause angst; and none of us escapes the sorrow and grief that assails us when the death of those whom we love deals us a body blow. Even when we rationalize "it was a blessing," the sadness of loss is ameliorated only gradually – if ever – and only after much time has transpired. When a death personally affects us, our instincts

*This is a curious expression of somewhat hermetic origins. Some conceive that it refers to kicking away the bucket from under the feet of a victim in the hangman's noose, others believe it refers to the gibbet on which slaughtered animals were hung to cure and catch the blood in a bucket. Still some believe it refers to the pail of holy water medieval clerics placed at the feet of a dying person so that the faithful could sprinkle them.

are to commemorate, recall and remember the person in some way, often emblematically. All societies through the ages have created symbolic themes that connote the end of the human condition and the grief it inflicts. For the most part, the iconographic emblems serve to ease the pain of survivors by honoring the loved one, and incidentally subdue the universal fear of death and the anxiety associated with the mystery of the unknown. It is iconography grounded in belief of an afterlife seeking meaning of life and bowing to the final curtain call of the *theatro vitae*.

♣

Classical Commemorative Iconography

Although memorials to adults often reflected philosophical acceptance of the inevitability of death with a focus on the individual's achievements or virtues, a wealth of allegorical iconography survived to highlight the manifold emotions the subject of death induces (Table 6).* Beginning with the Patristic period (100-450 CE) and after, in the early Middle Ages, classical beliefs shifted to the Christian *memento mori*,† an admonition that preparing for a "good death" was essential for salvation and the only *raison d'être* of man.[1] From the Renaissance on, artists infused their works, adhering to Church teachings, with moral lessons and reminders of the fragility of life, inevitable death and the fate that awaited errant souls.

Classical iconography of mortality in general was rich, reverent, complex and sometimes beautifully depicted; at other times, it intended to arouse trepidation, such the image of Atropos of the three Fates who cuts the thread of life, or the boatman Charon, who, as mentioned, rowed souls across the River Styx to Hades. Commonly found on stelae and sarcophagi of adults were images of doors or curtains that represented the passage into the next world. Figures were supine or standing, wearing the chin straps (*othonai*)

---

*In the classical civilizations of Greece and Rome, death iconography emerged that referred to children. The many decorative stelae that are extant depict specific attributes of childhood: toys, puppies, birds and fruit, all sentimental and innocent conceits of childhood (Table 7). Depictions of a Roman *conclamatio*, the Three Fates, the crossing of the Styx and Persephone were also depicted in child commemorations.

† Introduced in Chapter One on Religious Iconography.

that kept closed the mouths of the dead. Urns that held the ashes of the cremated for all to see at death *symposia* (funeral gatherings) had images of the Three Fates or of Charon. Dionysian or Bacchant images that honored and celebrated life were common representations on terracotta vases, *pinakes* and sarcophagi.[2] Mythology lives on!

The thread of life is a theme associated with the Greek *Moirae* (the Fates), three sisters traditionally depicted as old women robed in white who determined human fate. Lachesis sang of things that were and apportioned one's lot in life. Clotho sang of things that are and spun the thread of one's life span as measured by Lachesis, who also determined the length of an individual's life. Atropos intoned about things to come, and it was she who cut the thread of life. When Charon asked Hermes, "But what is that crowd of shapes that flies about the [the dead] unseen?" Hermes replied, that among them are the gods of fear, ignorance, anger, and hatred. If you look closely, you will also see the Fates up above, drawing off each man's thread from the spindle...."[3]

Fig. 128. Francesco Salviati. *The Three Fates.*

Thus, the Fates were held responsible when a young life was extinguished prematurely. Many tomb inscriptions spoke of *mors immature*. Quintilian (35-96 CE), for example, lamented the death of his son in the panegyric *Institutio Oratoriae*, in which he remembered "his [son's] first flashes of promise." Martial (40-104 CE) bitterly blamed his son's premature death on the Fates: "Buried am I here...Urbicus, an infant....Six months were wanting of my first three years when the harsh Goddesses cruelly snapt my thread" (*Epigrams*). A Roman sarcophagus, ca. 240 (Fig. 129), titled "Prometheus" by Louvre curators, shows the Greek Titan creating Man. It is understood in mythology that the fates of the many children who crowd the scene are determined by the *Moirae*. The helmeted Athena is on the left; Hermes follows, wearing his winged *petasus*. Next are two women, presumed to be the Fates Lachesis and Clotho, forever spinning a yarn about life. Poseidon, who has his trident in hand and Artemis, with her moon crescent, appears to be looking at a woman thought to be Atropos (without scissors), who nevertheless ominously rests a hand on the shoulder of a woman.

Fig. 129. Roman sarcophagus with *The Three Fates* (c. 100 AD).

The theme in Sophocles' *Antigone* explores the Greek obligation to honor the dead with a decent burial to ensure passage of the soul or psyche to an eternal home. No funeral, no ride on Charon's boat to Hades. Instead, 100 years of wandering up and down the river Styx in no man's land. Creon, the King of Thebes, orders the dead body of Polyneices to remain as carrion fodder unburied in the battlefield. The tragedy unfolds when Antigone defies her father's ignominious decree that disgraces and dooms her brother, and ceremoniously, in keeping with traditional burial rituals that honored the dead, proceeds with the first ritual – the laying out of the body, the *prothesis*.*

In ancient Greece, funerals were elaborate rites faithfully observed. Mourners assembled at the *prothesis* to show their respect and to express

*Creon arrests Antigone and she kills herself in prison.

145

their sorrow and grief. They remained present as the body was washed, anointed with oil and dressed in funereal garments. Lamentations were assured by several women hired for the occasion who followed the funeral procession, often with a musical accompaniment, as the bereaved lumbered forwards to the *ekphora* burial site where the body or cremated remains were interred. Mementos, food and flowers were placed into the grave. Memorial tombs, stelae and statues were erected to ensure the loved one would be remembered, thereby granting a sense of immortality. Depictions of death scenes were painted on terracotta *pinake* (Fig. 130), often with inscriptions of grief and lamentations such as *oimoi*, the modern equivalent of "woe is me." The Romans conformed more or less to Greek practice at funerals, but as Roman mourners stood around the bier of the dead, they intoned a ritual of their own devising called a *conclamatio* – they shouted out the name of the deceased three times (Fig. 131). Images of a *conclamatio* were frequently incised on sarcophagi. Common to depictions from both cultures was the likeness of a body reclined, at rest. The Greeks placed chin-straps (*othonai*) to keep the mouth closed. Symbolically, when a figure appears with *othonai*, regardless of the setting, the figure is of a dead individual. In Roman *conclamatio* scenes, the dead were depicted on a couch, or *triclinium* (Greek: *kline*) (Figs. 131 and 132). Even in the absence of a funeral gathering, a figure sculpted on a *kline* was interpreted as being dead. The iconographic image dates to the Etruscan period when couples were frequently depicted recumbent in death on the lids of sarcophagi (Fig. 133). Other imagery associated with death was commonly seen on sarcophagi, such as poppies (symbol of Hypnos and eternal sleep), Dionysian fruit and garlands or strigillated patterns. Greek and Roman mourners shown on sarcophagus reliefs depicted with covered heads or hands poised on the head referenced the profound grief of the loss of both children and adults.

Fig. 130. *Prosthesis* on Black figure pinax. (WC).

146

Fig. 131. Child sarcophagus with *conclamatio* 2nd c CE. Agrigento Temple Valley. (AP).

Fig. 132. Child sarcophagus with *conclamatio* (c. 100 CE). Cluny. (AP).

Fig. 133. Etruscan couple on cinerary urn lid (6th c. BCE). Louvre (AP)

147

The dead in ancient Greece were interred with a coin (*obol*) on the lips to pay the ferryman. Psychopomp Hermes (Roman: Mercury) led souls of the departed to Kahron (Roman: Charon). Once the *obol* was paid,* the soul could be transported across the river Styx to Hades. Illustrations of this custom are common on Greek pottery, but usually depicted on funereal offertory oil vessels, the *lekythos*. Painted white, they generally incorporated three essential elements: the soul waiting for transport, Charon with his boat and the shore of Hades. The soul was electively painted as plain folk or as an *eidolon*, a winged stick-figure that signified the soul being released from a body. This imagery was used equally for adult and child. The first of two *lekythos* examples shown here depicts Kahron and the Hermes, and the second shows Hypnos and Thanatos carrying Sarpedon from the Troy battlefield (Figs. 134 and 135). Hovering over Sarpedon's body is his winged *eidolon.*

The Roman name for Hermes was Mercury. A psychopomp, who led souls to the world of the dead, he is often portrayed partially hidden behind other icons of death – the door or the curtain. Usually depicted on sarcophagi, these attributes suggested that souls entered the netherworld through a portal lying just behind a door or curtain (Fig. 136). This portal represented the Roman concept of a new existence, as expressed by Horace (65-8 BCE): "I shall not altogether die, but a mighty part of me shall escape the death-goddess."

Psychopomps were culturally diverse. The Egyptians had the god *Anubis*, and the Etruscans, *Vanth*. Hinduism turned to Shiva as *Tarakeswara*. In Judaism and Islam, *Azrael* led the souls to peace. While *Charon, Hermes* and *St. Michael* are no longer invoked as psychopomps, Dava Sobel observes that the planet Mercury flees from light into darkness within an hour, making him the ideal psychopomp. The *Grim Reaper* is still with us. And get this: you can get certified to be an "End of Life Doula," a midwife for cutting the thread of life.

*Lucian of Samosata (120-190 CE), in his *Dialogues of the Dead*, with a reference to the *obol*, presciently presages the *vanitas* of the Renaissance: Charon says to Hermes: "You see what they [mortals] do and how ambitious they are, competing with each other over offices, honors and possessions, all of which they will be obliged to leave behind them when they come down to us with just one *obol*."

Fig. 134. Lekythos with
Charon and Hermes.

Fig. 135. Lekythos with Hypnos,
Thanatos and an eidolon.

The portal, however, also could be the entrance to hell through a cave. In the story of Orpheus and Eurydice, the entrance to Hades, or the Stygian realm (Fig. 39), was through a cave, an image clearly depicted by Michelangelo (1475-1564) in the *Last Judgment.* Charon ferries souls towards hell, while demons are seen hovering inside the cave opening to hell. The door to Hades was not depicted on child memorials.

Fig. 136. Sarcophagus with a doorway. *Four Seasons.* (c. 100 BCE).

Like other pagan concepts, Christians transmuted the notion so that by the medieval period the portal clearly referred to a door to heaven. In *John* 10:9, Christ called himself a door – "I am the door; whosoever enters by me shall be saved." The left triptych panel of *The Last Judgment* by Hans Memling (c. 1433-1494) (Fig. 138) depicts a line of faithful awaiting passage through the door.

Fig. 137. Memling. Doors to heaven (detail).

150

Fig. 138. Michelangelo. *Last Judgment* (detail).

Fig. 139. Stele for Apollonia.

Fig. 140. *Maiden holding a dove.*

Eschatological mythology interestingly held on tight to mortal life as evidenced in the apologue about Persephone, the consort of Hades, whom you may recall was given a pomegranate seed to eat before departing Hades. The seed, emblem of rebirth,* ensured her cyclical return to the underworld. Thus Persephone was viewed as a symbol of reincarnation, and her attribute, naturally enough, was the pomegranate. Stelae, particularly for girls, commonly featured the emblem. One example is of Apollonia from Thebes (Fig. 139). She stands in a three-quarter frontal position on the right of the stone. Her hair has a central braid typical of Greek girls in the 1st century, BCE. The age of the subject is not known, but the inscription on the stele clearly indicates it is a child. She strokes a dove, one of the Hellenistic attributes of a child, and she holds the tell tale pomegranate in the other hand.

---

*Incidentally, medieval midwives placed a pomegranate seed in the vagina of a parturient to assure a safe and rapid birth.

The bird made an appearance on Graeco-Roman funerary art, attributes that conveyed naturalness, elusiveness and the soul or life-force (Fig. 140). Birds were sculpted, held in the hands of children, and skeletal remains of birds have been found in graves of children. They were considered appropriate attributes because, like the *eidolon*, they were winged, and could fly and move between the spheres of the living and the dead. Plutarch (?46-120 CE), in *Consolation to his Wife*, compared the soul of his dead two-year-old daughter to a captive bird. Most often, Greek children were buried apart from their parents in partitioned cemetery areas. Common grave gifts were feeding bottles, dolls and clay-modeled pets. The iconographic significance of these items changed once they were buried; no longer toys, they became commemorative offerings to be used by the child in the next world.

There are few extant classical era Syrian stelae for children. The attributes are similar to those found in Greece. One, of a boy, Ma'nai, from the 2nd century CE, depicts him holding a bird and fruit (Fig. 141). The Aramaic inscription reads: "Ma'nai son of Iarhibola ... Alas!"[4] The symbol of fruit as an attribute in the hands of children in death remains speculative. Certainly fruit resonates as a source of nourishment, an object of pleasant distraction, or as sweet persuasion for a child, and it may be fruit was depicted simply as a general attribute of childhood. The later seems most likely, since fruit depicted in art remained an attribute of childhood until the Victorian period.

Fig. 141. *Stele of Syrian Boy* (2nd cent. CE). (AP)

153

Fig.142. *Bibliographic Sarcophagus of a Roman Child* (1st c. CE). (AP)

Rich Romans commemorated their deceased progeny with marble busts, reliefs and sarcophagi. A particularly fine example, rich in iconography, is biographical in its theme. A small 1st century CE marble sarcophagus, now in the Louvre (Fig. 142), depicts a tableau relief that relates the short life of a child from the father's perspective. Pictorially, the man wistfully gazes on the infant as a suckling and holds his child. Poignantly, the child is depicted riding in his toy chariot and finally, the bereft father, seated, gazes towards the figure of his child who clasps what appears to be a scroll. An iconological analysis of the sarcophagus is possible because of what is known of the social and cultural customs of Rome at the time. Amongst the well-to-do, those who could afford such a fine sarcophagus, a child was tended by a *nutrix* or wet-nurse for instance, and therefore the woman depicted was probably not the mother. In Rome, the ritual acceptance of a child was marked by the custom of *tollere,* when the father took the child in arms and raised it up as a sign of its legitimate place in the family. The boy in the toy chariot, a poignant reminder of happy fun filled days, is doubtlessly the child who died. In the final sequence, the child is prematurely garbed in the *toga virum* in the posture and gesture of rhetoric, and holds a scroll in a declamatory position, a metaphorical reference to unrealized potential. The father, who clasps a scroll of authority, looks at the boy with an expression that reveals a gamut of emotions – pride, admiration, sadness and woe. One can speculate he is cogitating about the lost potential of his son. The images prove the point of that old chestnut a picture is worth a thousand words, as in this touching biography of a beloved and profoundly mourned son prematurely taken from this earth.

Roman memorials with inscriptions and figures in relief were common. Some included the entire family. One example from Museo Capitolio in Rome depicts the father, mother and child. The boy wears a *toga pueris,* a student's toga, and a *bulla,* an amulet that only freeborn boys could wear (Fig. 143). The mother offers the child fruit, symbol of eternal abundance, from a basket. Two birds, the symbol of the life force, face the boy in profile.

Fig. 143. *Grave Marker of a Roman Family* (2nd cent. AD). Museo Capitolio. (AP).

♣

Medieval, Renaissance and Baroque Death Iconography

In the Christian West, the Patristic period marked the beginning of intense monastic scholarship that produced parchment manuscripts and exquisite illuminated volumes that were carefully preserved in scriptoriums. Magnificently illustrated books of prayer and books on rituals for the dead that placed emphasis on salvation of the soul were also painstakingly produced. Generally speaking, the monastic iconography mutated from the celebration of life, the *carpe diem*, to reminders of death, the *memento mori*, and the imperative of the faithful to attain spiritual salvation. By the 15th century, penitence and deliverance became dominant themes in art, and thus, during this period, references to children and children's deaths all but disappeared. The remarkable iconography of death had begun to refer only to adults, and it reflected the apprehensions and fears of the faithful and their anxiety ridden hope for a "Good Death," a Christian passing that would lead them to the right hand of God.

With Christianity, classical themes of death were viewed with opprobrium, and either abandoned as pagan or altered to conform to Christian concepts. By the end of the millennium, a new and different iconography had emerged to commemorate death, despite instances where ancient roots remained apparent. The pomegranate became a conceit of resurrection, Charon's boat became the Ship of Salvation, mourners became hooded monks or innocent *orphelins*, the dove became the Holy Spirit, and

Archangel Michael became the psychopomp. The *gisant* retained the postures common to reclined Roman figures, but symbols had acquired Christian connotations, such as the *gisant* with hands devoutly folded in prayer (Fig. 144) or reading a book of hours. Valentine Balbani, sculpted by Germain Pilon (c. 1537-1590), embodies the style (Fig. 145). To us she looks more saucy than devout as she peruses a book in a semi-recumbent position on the lid of the tomb. Ingeniously, Pilon also depicted her below, in the tomb, in relief, as a *transi*, lest one forget what death looks like.

Orphelins or orphans came to be identified as mourners, because to raise sums to support older children, hospices depended on revenues raised from "renting-out" their charges to participate in funeral processions. It seems that status commonly was measured by the numbers in a funeral cortege. Wealthy families were willing to pay to have a train of children, dressed in the uniforms of their hospices, follow the coffins of their deceased. In France, the children of the Hôpital Enfants Rouge wore red, those of Saint-Espirit wore blue, and those of the Hôpital des Orphelins wore gray.

Fig. 144. Bartarnay gisants in prayer, Montrésor*

*Note the *gisant* of M. Batarnay wears a chain of office crafted in the design of scallop shells. Whose conceit? Hmmm –Table one will reveal all.

Fig 145. Pilon.Tombeau Valentine Balbiari with breviary.

The Transi

Classical funereal representations of peaceful figures recumbent on their tombs usually shown as youthful and beautiful, and, much to the satisfaction of those still living with inferences that their entry into the afterlife had succeeded, did not altogether vanish in the Christian world. But how on earth did the *transi* image still seen in great cathedrals originate and become a common – and terrifying – sight? The speculation is that the reoccurring epidemics that decimated the population of Europe precipitated an eschatological preoccupation in the Middle Ages that most likely inspired the iconography of the *transi*. The staggering numbers of deaths called for quick burials. In order to make way for fresh internments, human bones from exhumed graves were transferred to charnel houses. Tales told by grave diggers* would have fueled fear of plague-borne disease and sudden death among the general populace that generated traumatized impressions

---

*A fractured staff in paintings signified death (see Figure 113). The conceit evolved from the common practice in graveyards of placing a measuring rod besides the corpse, indicating to the grave digger the length of the body to be buried. Customarily after the measurement, the rod, long a walking aid during difficult journeys, was broken as a symbol that a person's spiritual journey had ended (see Figure 170 and note the little figure just to the right of the hourglass). In *The Tempest*, Shakespeare references it: Prospero: "I'll break my staff, bury it certain fathoms in the earth." V, I, 54-56. A body sewn into a white linen sack – a shroud – assumed symbolic meaning in parts of the Christian world, signaling the deceased was a saved soul, one who had confessed all sins to a priest and had been given absolution – the forgiveness of sins.

of macabre images of partially decomposed mortal remains and human bones. Artistic images such as the *transi* on tombs conveniently reinforced the Church's message of *memento mori.*

In the early 1300s, Dutch and German iconography evolved the topos of *Fürst der Welt* that believed the world was evil, with sinful temptation a constant peril.   Statues appeared on cathedrals façades that depicted the duality of the Prince of Darkness. A frontal view of *Fürst der Welt* showed a handsome man with a comforting smile.   The rear view, however, depicted the body corrupting, decomposing, evolving into a *transi.* Three illustrations below are from Nürnberg (1310), Strasbourg (1400) and Worms (1298). The interpretation was clear to all: the beauty of the body did not last; death and decay was everyone's destiny, with eternal damnation the fate of those who succumbed to sinful temptations and vanity.   This iconography influenced artists in the 15th century to depict man in death as a mummified decomposing body, called a *transi*, a *memento mori.*

Fig. 146. *Fürst der Welt* (front and rear). Nürnberg.

158

Fig. 147. *Fürst der Welt*, Strasbourg.   Fig. 148. *Fürst der Welt*, (front and rear) Worms.

The revolting *transi* was intended to horrify and shock an orant to repent and inspire a lifelong devotion to prayer, supplication and penance in order to merit heavenly salvation. The commemorative tombs that depicted the deceased as a *transi*, with tattered remains of linen clinging to bones, also were most likely inspired by mummified bodies that had been exhumed in parish graveyards in which soil conditions preserved bodies. In St. Michel in Bordeaux and St. Bonnet-le-Chateau in Loire, parchment-like bodies were found in the clay soil of church cemeteries. Mummies from these parishes most likely served as the models for medieval artists who portrayed these gruesome figures of souls who awaited their final judgment.

Certainly, for medieval northern Europe the depiction of death as a corpse undergoing decomposition was a graphic Christian reminder of the ultimate return to earth as dust. These decaying – and decayed – bodies, depicted with putrefying flesh and organs clinging to them, were *en transi*, awaiting the Last Judgment. They were infested with snakes, toads and creatures of carrion. Striking examples survive. Arguably the most brilliant is the Tomb of Rene of Chalon, Prince of Orange, by Ligier Richier (1500-1567) – a student of Michelangelo. The artist integrated irony with *vanitas* as the astonishing skeletal *transi* complacently stares into a heart-shaped mirror, a symbol of the topos (Fig. 149). The great and mighty liked to leave memorials of themselves as *transi* – a questionable gesture of humility that

159

may have been subconscious acknowledgement of the immoral lives they had lead. The powerful and scheming Catherine de Medici was sculpted supine, wasted, with sagging breasts and loose skin clinging to bone, in consort as a *transi* with her pitiful looking spouse, the French king Henry II, in the Basilica of St. Denis in Paris (Fig. 150). John Fitzalan, Earl of Arundel (1223–1267), is seen in the powerful garb of a knight, but, tellingly, below he lies in state as a *transi* (Fig. 151).*

Fig. 149. Rene de Chalon, Bar-le-Duc, France.

*Although not shown here, we call attention to modern artists' work while on the subject of *memento mori*. Damien Hirst (b. 1965), among other postmodern conceptualists, is an example. Hirst's *A Thousand Years*, with a rotting cow's head, flies, maggots and decaying flesh can readily be conceptually viewed as a modern secular *transi*. The dead shark in *The Physical Impossibility of Death* and the diamond-studded platinum skull of *For the Love of God* repeat the *vanitas* motif, intentionally or not.

Fig. 150. Henri II and Catherine De Medici, St. Denis.

Fig. 151. John Fitzalan, West Sussex.

Very often the *transi* were emblazoned with Latin banderoles with dictums such as "We are born to die daily, I am what you will be" or "Contemplate this." So striking was the *transi* as a pedagogical model for penitence, that free-standing depictions were placed in churches. Now in the Museo Nacional de Escultura, Valladolid, the magnificent *memento mori* wooden sculpture of Gil de Ronza (1483-1535) as a *transi* holds the trumpet that summons all to the final judgment. For centuries it was in the church of San Francisco in Valladolid.

Fig. 152. Ronza. *La Muerte* (1523)

The Skeleton

As must be apparent in the above examples, in time, artists' renderings of the *transi* exaggerated the degree of decomposition until these figures were represented as "*morte secca*" – dried out skeletons – not in the medieval *Danse Macabre* tradition of representations of corrupt behavior, but in the sense of the Christian theme of "dust thou art and to dust thou shall return." Frequently abbreviated to a skull with cross-bones (generally femurs), the bones became the paradigm of the *memento mori*. These osseous artifices appeared everywhere – in books, paintings, monuments, buildings. No European could travel anywhere without confronting skeletal death as *memento mori*. Even in offices, hovering over the conduct of business, the intrusion of the image prevailed. Stripped of all physiognomy,

162

the skeleton and empty skull with dark voids for eye sockets and cavernous boney nostrils evoked fear and horror, and served as a multifaceted tool to promulgate the message of "prepare, for ye know not when or where" in monuments, tombstones, breviaries, and, particularly, in the themes of *The Three Living and the Three Dead,* the *Danse Macabre* or *Todtentanz, Death Triumphant* and *Ars moriendi.*

Fig.153. Entrance to St. Olaf's Chapel, Amsterdam (c. 1440).
"In the next life there is hope" (AP).

Fig. 154. Jacob van Campen Ceremonial Office
Royal Palace Amsterdam (AP).

Even in textbooks of new anatomical studies made possible by edicts of the Council of Trent which sanctioned dissection, the skeleton assumed eschatological significance. In Vesalius's (1514-1564) *De Fabrica Humani Corporis* (1543) – with plates by Steven Kalcar (1500-1546), a student of Titian – a whimsical skeleton stands, legs rakishly crossed, pondering a skull. Death meditating on death; it is amusing, satirical and a graphic *memento mori* reminder of the inevitable. True to his anatomical genius, Vesalius's rendering of the underside of the human skull on the pedestal is drawn in perfect detail.

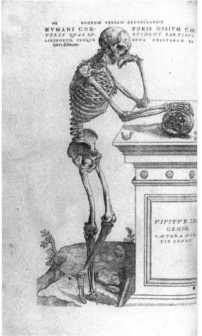

Fig. 155. Kalcar. Vesalius' *De Corpore*.

Scholar de Jongh has commented on the "inductive" effects of the skull in a painting. It is such a powerful symbol of death that everything else in a work of art devolves to a mere *vanitas* symbol. Thus, in Adriaen van Utrecht's (1599-1652) *Still Life*, the flowers, coins, nautilus, pearls, books, sundial, etc. serve as *vanitas* metaphors for the iconographical skull *memento mori*.

164

Fig. 156. van Utrecht. *Still Life* (1642).

♣

Like it or not, feminists, a beautiful woman is a *vanitas* symbol. On balance, Death is often shown as a *transi*-skeleton and is always a predatory male. What a *memento mori*! A Maiden and Death, often shown in a Kiss of Death – a *Mors osculi*. The *Mors osculi* and the *vanitas* theme joined forces in the hands of several artists, in works such as those of Hans Baldung Grien (c 1485-1545), who was fond of employing multiple symbols in one work. His painting, *Mors osculi* (Fig. 157), evokes the customary horror of the theme, but curiosity as well. It is not clear if the woman in the painting is disrobing or if she is donning a shroud. Her expression reflects repulsion, terror and resignation in this repugnant image of a lovely young woman being seduced by death. Grien's painting incorporates a medieval attribute of death – the cloven foot of a horned devil of death referred to in the Book of Revelations (4: 6). In a version of *Mors osculi* (Fig. 158) by Niklaus Manuel Deutsch (? 1484-1530) the seduction is flagrant, and the more alarming for it.

Fig. 157. Grien. *Death and the Maiden-Mors Osculi.*

Fig. 158. Nicklaus Manuel. *Mors Osculi*

Italian humanists perceived *mors osculi* or *bacio di morte* as archetypical. The Kiss of Death (generally, but not exclusively) on the mouth alluded to the release of the soul from the mouth at the moment of death, effected by a lethal kiss, considered a mystical transfer of the soul from this world. In *Death and the Maiden (*Fig. 159*)* Death ominously holds an iconic hourglass over a lovely woman clearly enraptured by her reflection in a mirror. It is Grien's interpretation of the Ages of Man topos: *Infantia* is the child, the man is *vir* and the young woman appears as *iuvenis*. The mirror, it should be noted, remains even today one of the most immutable of *vanitas*–death symbols. Both of Grien's paintings belong to the complex subtext of the Eros-Thanatos theme (the sacrificial aspect of love).[5] The sagacious optical illusion of an image of a skull in *All is Vanity* (Fig. 160) by C. Alan Gilbert (1873-1929) conveys the *vanitas/memento mori* theme of a beautiful woman admiring herself in a boudoir mirror in a unique and original way.

Fig. 159. Grien. *Death and the Maiden.*

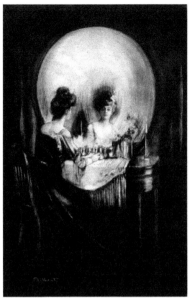

Fig. 160. Gilbert. *All is Vanity.*

In medieval times a new mythology evolved that had no super-heroes or avenging gods, but was rooted in Church decrees on matters of morality, mortality and salvation. The story of *The Three Living and the Three Dead*, a legend that first appeared in French poems written in the 13th century, was a precursor to the allegory of the *danse macabre*, known also as *Todtentanz* in which the skeletal dead lead the living, from pope to peasant to the great equalizer, death. The tale relates the story of three noblemen – a duke, a count and a son of the king – who, while riding in a field, come across a cemetery hidden by overgrowth. They are startled by the sudden appearance of three dead beings in transitional states of decay and skeletal decomposition. The three dead men narrate their tales. The first says in life he was a pope, the second says he was a cardinal, and the third relates he was notary to the pope. They all warn, "you will become as we are; in anticipation, mirror yourselves in us; power, honor, riches are nothing; only good works count at the hour of death."[6] The legend was a widespread popular narrative, and, as the topic of church frescoes, in breviaries as accompaniments to the poem, although uncommon, are extant. With the story intact, by the end of the 15th century, it had become a legend of three young men on horseback who are hunting when the three dead figures startle them (Fig. 161). The tale in both versions ends positively: having been forewarned, the three determine to live lives of virtue, good works and modesty to merit eternal blessings.

Fig. 161. *Three Living and Three Dead.*

Fig. 162. Holbein. *Todtentanz.*

In a series of woodcuts (1526), Hans Holbein the younger (1497-1543), in a deviation from the traditional representation of a parade of figures of the *danse macabre*, depicts individuals from all stations of life to great dramatic effect. A small child (Fig. 162) being snatched away from his parents by skeletal Death is a wrenching example. The skeleton that led the *dramatis personae* of the *Dance Macabre* probably first appeared in France

169

as a morality play towards the end of the 14th century. The characters, personages marching in hierarchical order, follow a skeleton hand in hand towards death. There are typically twenty-four subjects in all, among them a king, pope, cardinal, bishop, knight, physician, lawyer, merchant, farmer, mother, and child. No one escapes death. Each gives a recitation during the journey. The bishop, for example, declaims, "I walk toward death whether I like it or not; I leave behind the cross, sandals and miter." The knight laments, "I walk toward death. I have won many a contest, but I have not learned to win over death." The text of French quatrains is attributed to Lyonnais Jean de Vauzelles or Gilles Corrozet, inspired by the book of *Job*. "I, who, conceiv'd in the dark womb, into the world is brought, born to times with misery and various evil fraught." This dramatic and dreadful association of death with the living grew as a popular theme throughout Europe. Delatinized into the *lingua franca*, it was called *Danse Macabre, Todtentanz,* and *Danza general de la muerte*. Although introduced into Italy, it gained no popularity in a land where the *transi* was uncommon, and where popes, cardinals and bishops often owed their status to nepotism, and self-indulgence was more a guiding principal than interest in helping others achieve salvation. These icons of reminders of mortality, inspired numerous woodcut depictions, breviary miniatures, paintings, and church murals. There is evidence the faithful regarded them with fear and trembling. A fragment of the work by Bernt Notke (1435-1509) can be seen in St. Nicolas Church in Tallinn (Fig. 163).

Fig. 163. Fragment of *Dance Macabre* by Notke in St. Nicolas, Tallin, Estonia

The topos of the Dance of Death embodied two absolutes: it is indiscriminate and often unforeseen and therefore allows no opportunity for repentance that brings salvation. This unbearably shocking visual and literary convention, often rendered in stunningly horrifying images, was bound to generate a backlash, and, in the second half of the 15th century, less than a hundred years after the Black Death claimed up to sixty percent of the world's population, a more optimistic concept of *memento mori* evolved that offered Christian comfort and emphasized redemption as the reward for penitence. The new, instantly popular theme was introduced in a small book, *Ars moriendi* – the art of a good death. *Ars moriendi* was published in two versions in 1415 and in 1450. The early version was written by a Dominican. Four of its six chapters offer hope and reassurances that dying is not to be feared; advises how to resist the five temptations aroused as death approaches; offers consolation that redemption is possible through Christ's love and advocates an imitation of the life of Christ. The last two chapters give instructions on deathbed comportment for family and friends and offer the appropriate deathbed prayers. The shorter 1450 version focuses on how to withstand the five temptations. Early versions in France and then throughout Europe of the more than twenty editions had woodblock prints. They were among the first incunabulum printed with block wood woodcuts. Late editions were richly illustrated with depictions such as a man on his death bed confronted by the five final temptations as personified figures, iconographic monsters with identifying lettered banderoles spewing from their mouths – doubt, despair, blasphemy, avarice and pride. Through prayer and meditation, man defeats the devils and demons and thereby attains salvation. In every edition the final saga includes the image of an angel carrying off the man's soul (depicted iconographically as a child), to his heavenly reward. Considered the most beautiful illustrations of the *Ars moriendi* are those depicted in *Rohan's Book of Hours* (Fig.164). The man in extremis, is nude, in a cemetery surrounded by scattered bones. He lies on a fine blue and gold brocaded shroud as the last breath from his mouth, in the form of a banderole, has a resigned message written on it in Latin, "Into your hands I commend my spirit," echoing Christ's dying words from the cross. In the background, a demon is engaged in battle with a determined St. Michael the Archangel who aims to wrest the child soul of the man from the grip of the devil. The kindly deity assures the dead man in a banderole written in French, "This day you shall be in paradise with me." The representation of the child as a soul that had become part of the iconography of death in the Renaissance was based on the concept of the child as an innocent, and a belief that the soul begins life anew in the kingdom of God. The theme remained popular until the beginning of the 19th century. The handsome illuminated books now grace the museums of Europe.

Fig. 164. *Ars moriendi*. Rohan Hours.

Fig. 165. Anon. *Bestiary* Hyena (13th c.).

172

Beasts of carrion became symbolic of death. Hyenas and wild dogs were depicted gnawing on putrefying bodies, and vultures spiraled around the dead (Fig. 165). These images appeared in breviaries and as manuscript marginalia, serving as *memento mori*. Gaunt animals feeding on the dead also appeared in *Death Triumphant*, another gruesome reminder of the impartiality and inevitability of death.

In literature and art the raven became a symbol of death. Lady Macbeth, regarding the death of Duncan, says, "The raven himself is hoarse/ That croaks the entrance of Duncan." (Act I: 5). In a letter to her father, Galileo (1564-1642), Suor Maria Celeste (1600-1634) comments, "...it devolves upon me to play the raven who bears bad tidings, as I must tell you ...Goro died."[7] In Brueghel's masterpiece, *Triumph of Death* (Fig. 166), the raven accompanies skeletal Death on horseback as he makes his rounds.

The topos of *Triumphus mortis* or *Death Triumphant* dates back to the early *trecento* (14th century Italian culture). It is based on the dictum "*mors certa, hora incerta*," and the first known fresco depiction is in a cycle in the Camposanto of Pisa by Buonamico Buffalmacco (fl 1315-1356) Fig. 167. On one side, the fresco depicts nobles and courtesans engaged in a summer hunt who come across *transi* in their coffins. (This iconography linking courtly love with death conforms to the aforementioned Eros-Thanatos theme). On the right side of the fresco, angels and demons, flying over heaps of dead, compete for souls. Reminiscent of the *Three Living and the Three Dead*, the scale of the work as well as the imagery are psychologically more complex and powerful as death comes universally, indiscriminately and cruelly.

Fig. 166. Brueghel. *The Triumph of Death* (detail).

Fig. 167. Buonamico Buffalmacco. *The Triumph of Death* (1330).

174

Prescient and uncannily apropos, Buffalmacco's *Triumphus mortis*, painted circa 1330, predates the catastrophic Black Plague by seventeen years. Giovanni Boccaccio (1313-1375), in his classic work (completed in 1353) *The Decameron*, (a compilation of a hundred entertaining tales told by a small group who have escaped the plague in a sequestered villa outside of Florence) mentions the famous fresco, suggesting the visionary's work was widely known. After the devastation and societal upheaval of the plague, the *memento mori* references in the painting would have had enormous resonance for woeful survivors that ruefully understood too well the frightening vulnerability and fragility of life and the horrors that could be visited upon them. This stunning awareness inspired artists for hundreds of years.

The most famous – unforgettable – depiction of *triumphus mortis**
was realized by Pieter Brueghel, the Elder (c.1525-1569) in 1562 (Fig. 168). Copies made by his sons Pieter and Jan ensured the work received widespread recognition. Brueghel the Elder combined two thematic traditions, the Italian *Trionfo della morte* and the northern *Todtentanz*, to execute (literally) an apocalyptic world. The work is saturated with emblematic Death in the guise of an army of skeletons spiritedly, casually, committing heinous acts against humanity. Marching troops of skeletons destroy everyone in their path. For the viewer, it is both an exceptionally arresting colorful composition of great artistic merit and, in depicting people dressed in attire of the period, gives insight about people of the times, intensifying the horrific nightmare of seeing them murdered in every conceivable manner. The skeletons' skulls natural expressions appear cheery, escalating the sense of revulsion the scene evokes. Other symbols of death litter the gruesome genocidal scene. In one corner, a death bell is tolled; hanged bodies and corpses on gibbet wheels rot as vultures circle overhead. Death, with a symbolic raven besides him, holds an hourglass, a reminder of the ephemeral nature of life and a symbol of death. Astride a wasted white horse that pulls a wagon full of skulls ("... and I saw a white horse, and he who sat thereon his name was death." *Revelation* 6:8), Death brandishes a hand bell that mocks the customary call to "bring out your dead." Skeletal death with a scythe is there, driving hoards into a cross marked container like box. Fires. Ships sinking. Desperation in the faces of the few who remain alive makes one recoil. Children rarely are featured in apocalyptic scenes. Considered innocent and blameless, they were exempt from the wrath of God; but Brueghel spared no one from his vision of universal carnage.

*This is one painting that must be seen up close and in detail. Go to the Prado and study it. But, if you can't, check out Wikipedia Commons that has a high definition (5000 pixel) image which can be further enlarged revealing minutiae to match the sidereal heavens.

There are, surprisingly, two children in his work, one in the arms of a dead woman being menaced by a sniffing skeletal carnivorous dog, and a dead newborn lying in a coffin with its shrouded mother. Whatever happened to *ars moriendi*? It was so consoling, all that advice about the art of dying. Brueghel's painting makes Edvard Munch's *The Scream* appear ho-hum.

Fig. 168. Brueghel. *The Triumph of Death* (1562).

Hourglass

Not all iconography is as obvious in meaning as the skeleton; and the origins of other symbolic elements can be difficult to establish. A good example, germane to this discussion, is the hourglass. Although universally accepted as an icon of death, it is uncertain how and when this association evolved. Erwin Panofsky emphatically states that there is no hourglass in the representation of time in the persona of Kronos or Father Time, nor is there an image of an hourglass in antiquity, with the exception of a sandglass, an Alexandrian invention c.150 BCE. The first known hourglass is on a sarcophagus dated c. 350 CE (Amalfi Cathedral) that depicts the wedding of Peleus and Thetis and a sleeping Morpheus with the timepiece in his hands. Jump to 1338 to find another hourglass in art, in the hands of Temperance in Lorenzetti's *Allegory of Good Government* (see Fig. 17). The significance in that master work is somewhat ambiguous, but can be construed as a reference to the erosion of life by time and the need for temperance in all things. Ship records make mention of the hourglass as early as 1200s. They were the most dependable method to measure time at sea. Today, most of us think of it as a utilitarian 3-minute egg timer.

Only in the Renaissance did the hourglass acquire symbolic meaning in the West, and then undoubtedly as an established feature in the iconography of death. In Renaissance art, ancient mythology came into vogue, and the time measuring hourglass became one of several attributes associated with the god Saturn (Greek: Kronos). The relevance will become clear once you read their story. Saturn/Kronos were patrons of agriculture and carried a scythe (Fig. 169). Both devoured their children, a perversion more emphasized in Roman mythology: Saturn feared the prophesy his children from his union with Cybele would one day seize his power, so he cannibalized each one as they were born. Saturn/Kronos, in that both consumed that which they had created, became associated with Time which consumes all things. Metaphorically, Time is fleeting and passes quickly. Imagery evolved that depicted Kronos and Saturn with large, feathery wings, but Saturn had a much more sinister image as the cannibalistic scythe-wielding partner of Death who harvested human beings with his sickle. Elsewhere in art, in a far less sinister symbol, hourglasses were drawn with wings that supported the idea, as on the far left of *Symbols of Death* (Fig. 170), that Time "flies" and death is swift and certain.

Fig. 169. Ignaz Günther. *Chronos.*

Fig. 170. Jacob Matham after Karel van Mander. *Symbols of Death* (detail).

Homo bulla and other Death Iconography

After the figure of the skeleton, the most widely used symbol of mortality probably is *homo bulla*, an ancient emblem that refers to the fragility and transience of life in which man is compared to a translucent evanescent bubble. Charon, the Ferryman, speaks to Hermes, "Let me tell you, Hermes, what I think men and the whole life of man resemble. You have noticed bubbles in water caused by a streamlet splashing down....They burst without fail in time, for it cannot be otherwise. Such is the life of men...."[8] Generally without mention in the medieval period, during the Reformation the theme was resurrected, and it became a popular motif in painting, especially favored as a Dutch *vanitas*, and most commonly depicted in scenes of an innocent child blowing bubbles or watching bubbles rise and disappear in a silent burst – *in ictu oculi*. The engraving by Hendrick Goltzius (1558-1617) (Fig. 171) is more explicit: a putto leans on a skull while he blows bubbles. The smoking urn behind him, a symbol of death, complements the title, *Quis Evadet?* (Who will be spared?)

Satirist Lucian of Samosata (c.125-180 CE) wrote cutting and mocking dialogues that ridiculed beliefs of an afterlife. He admired Democritus, Epicurus and the Cynic philosopher Diogenes – all which comes through quite clearly in his *Dialogues of the Dead, Charon and the Inspector* and *Dialogues of the Gods*.

Fig. 171. Hendrick Goltzius. *Quis Evadet?*

Fig. 172. Alciati. *Terminus.*

The butterfly, like the bubble, symbolized transience. Fluttering away like ebbing life, it was a favorite emblem depicted alongside moribund flowers and empty shells in *vanitas* paintings. Imbedded as well in the symbol of the butterfly was the hope of transformation and resurrection. The product of the process of metamorphosis makes that interpretation a no-brainer. Some iconography, monumental in nature and uncommonly seen in paintings, was featured in sculptures. Terminus, *ouroboros*, smoking urns and the broken column are iconic examples (Fig. 172).

Terminus, the Roman deity who protected Roman borders, was depicted as a bust resting on a plinth at borders. On the feast of Terminalia (thought to be February 23), sacrificial blood was poured over the stone to strengthen its protective powers. Emblemata 157 of Andrea Alciati (1492-1550) refers to Terminus as an icon of death. The Latin reads, "The base of a squared shaft is firmly buried, and on top of it is a curly-haired image [of a man] cut off at the breast; this declares that he will yield to nobody. This is Terminus [the limit], the one goal that leads men on. It is the fixed day, and the time which has been set by the fates, and in the last events they render their judgment over the first day."[9] Thus the motto of Terminus, "*concede nulli*" (I yield to none) came to represent the unmovable, the predetermined, that which the fates ordained – death.

A snake swallowing its tail, the *ouroboros*, is an ancient symbol of eternal life. Snakes were believed to live forever. The sloughing of its skin was interpreted as rebirth, and the circle of its body a cycle without end. Except for hermetic eschatological manuscripts, the *ouroboros* fell into disuse during the ascendancy of Christianity. It reappeared in the Reformation, when Protestant churches divested itself of saintly images and icons of Mary and inserted secular images of resurrection. The tomb of Viscountess Doneraile (1671) depicts a child as a symbol of innocence, holding an *ouroboros*. The physiognomy is that of a latent boy, face puffed by weeping, with down-turned fish mouth sadness. He stands in slight contraposto, one hand clinging to a loincloth of modesty and the other with the *ouroboros*.

The ouroboros or uroborus has Egyptian roots. There are extant protective gnostic charms, such as this one (1st cent. CE) from the Walters Museum in Baltimore, which shows double emblems, the ouroboros on the outside and the sacred scarab on the inside, both invoking long life and resurrection. Magical script surrounds the scarab.

Fig. 173. Child holding an *ouroboros* (AP).

Fig. 174. Broken columns (AP).

The broken column is symbolic of life prematurely snapped, and, like the *ouroboros*, is a death symbol. Typically, a column is sculpted with a jagged mid-shaft, but on occasions, other death iconography accompanies it, such as the example in Figure 174 that displays a shroud and funereal garlands. A general preoccupation with death and salvation consumed Protestant Europe during the 16th to 18th centuries, an obsession that resulted in pervasive *memento mori* that were featured in works in churches and public monuments, in paintings and samplers and even in jewelry (Fig. 175). The objective of Reformation theology was to remind the faithful at every turn, in all endeavors, in all things, about death and the need for atonement.

In the 15th century, a common funereal icon was the image of a mourner. Life-size freestanding figures of hooded monks were placed around tombs. Some depicted on tomb slabs were posed ritualistically preparing the body, reading last rites, bent in sorrow. The example (Fig. 176) is by Pere Oller (fl. 1394-1442) from the tomb of Ferdinand I of Aragon.

Fig.175. *memento mori* ring (c.1600).   Fig. 176. Oller. *Mourner.*

With the Reformation and the revolt against monasticism, emergent Protestant Europe substituted a child or children for the role. Specifically, toddler or toddlers were depicted mourning the adult in death. Toddlers were grouped around monuments with faces contorted in grief, hands to chubby pouting faces, or holding *vanitas* icons, like the one from the church of Louis IX in Paris (Fig. 177).

182

Fig. 177. *Mourning Toddler* (AP).

Six cherub-like figures that grace the ceremonial office of the Amsterdam Royal Palace grieve and lament, *memento mori* reminders for those who conducted business there (Fig. 154). Two sit on a mantle and lean on a skull for support. Both wipe away tears. Two on the lateral decorative mullions, like the *conclamatio*, hold their heads in mournful disbelief. The last two stand, unable to confront the pain – one even turns his back in despair.

The putto-like figure on the monument to Countess Brandon (Fig. 178) stands on a sepulcher wiping his eyes with a shroud. Note that in this monument, the *homo totus* or *gisant* was replaced by the *imago clipeata* within a medallion. Sensitivities changed in the 18th century and commemoration by display of a *gisant* in rigor was no longer considered proper.

In the Western world, the bell, beginning in the 5th century AD, was at first used as a call to worship. By the 7th century, nearly every village in Europe had a bell-tower. It is known that the Venerable Bede (c. 673-735) used the bell not only to announce the hours of Compline, but also as a toll to announce a departed soul; in all probability a common practice. The use

---

The *Imagio clipeata* was not new. The Romans used the motif in depicting ancestral family trees, a reference noted by Pliny in his *Historia Naturalis*. By the 17th and 18th centuries, a portrait within a medallion came to denote apotheosis or salvation.

Fig. 178. *Countess Brandon* (AP).

of a bell knell to signal a death was most famously expressed in Meditation 17 of John Donne's (1573-1631) *Devotions Upon Emergent Occasions** In treasured prose Donne writes of bells: *"Nunc lento sonitu dicunt, morieris"* (now [these bells] softly tolling say, thou must die). The imagery of the bell with its soulful, muted tones that heralded a death became a fixed icon of mortality depicted on tombstones in the company of other icons. An 18th century tombstone in Scotland shows a skull, crossbones, hourglass, bell and a winged souls off to heaven – death iconography in its most economic, comprehensive and succinct form. Another tombstone from a Jewish cemetery in Poland displays winged hourglass.

Fig. 179. St. Fergus Kirkyard.

*No man is an island, entire of itself; every man is a piece of the continent, a part of the main. If a clod be washed away by the sea, Europe is the less, as well as if a promontory were, as well as if a manor of thy friend's or of thine own were: any man's death diminishes me, because I am involved in mankind, and therefore never send to know for whom the bells tolls; it tolls for thee.

184

Fig. 180. 18th c. tombstone, Powazki Jewish Cemetery.

Several symbols shared common properties: the extinguished candle, torch and spent rocket all referred to a life snuffed out. The smoke emitted from these and from urns was another reflection of extinguished life reaffirmed in the *Book of Psalms*, 102:3, "...for my days are consumed like smoke."

Vanitas

Vanitas paintings convey the message of inexorable death, the transient nature of life and the ephemeral character of all earthly triumphs and delights as a reminder to repent and redeem your soul in order to attain eternal peace. The theme has been referenced several times in this book since it has been famously employed in art. *Vanitas* paintings grace museums by the thousands and, although they have come to be associated with Dutch still lifes of the Golden Age, they were most commonly *memento mori* as early as the 1500s, intended to stun the viewer into reflecting on the state of the soul. In literature, 14th century Geoffrey Chaucer and William Langland immortalized the omnipresent theme. Morality plays of the 15th and 16th century and Shakespeare's several references kept their audiences' awareness current, most enduringly, Hamlet's soliloquy about his childhood jester, Yorick. William Makepeace Thackeray's (1811-1863) satirical novel, *Vanity Fair* (written 1847-48), may be the most well known of the 19th century literary references. His conniving heroine, Becky Sharp, could easily qualify as the beautiful nude woman seen in traditional *vanitas* images. A man of his times, Thackeray's character reflects the morals of the age, but his characterization conforms to the iconographic principles that the pursuit of earthly wealth, pleasures, knowledge and beauty are trivial and frivolous when weighed against the inevitability of death and the imperative to merit eternal salvation. Thackeray, as with many a moralist before him, concluded, "Ah! Vanitas Vanitatum! ...which of us is happy in this world? Which of us has his desire? Or, having it, is satisfied?" *Ecclesiastes* 1:2 says it best: "*Vanitatus et omnia vanitas* – vanity of vanities, all is vanity."

Depictions of *vanitas* as *memento mori* were on a par with those that symbolically emphasized the fragile, temporal and ephemeral value of

185

power and riches: jewels, gold, coins, musical instruments, books, flowers, exotica, gleaming glass cornucopia of foods, mirrors, shells, they all conveyed the message that death looms over all. From 1409 to 1963, as part of a pope's coronation rite, a Franciscan priest held up a pole with burning flax, extinguished it and incanted *"Pater santé, Sic transit Gloria mundi."* Indeed, even for popes, "thus passes the glory of the world."

Surely no other painting exemplifies the artistic expression of death and its iconography more than *L'Umana Fragilita* – Human Fragility (Fig.181) by Salvatore Rosa (1615-1673). It is a stunning expression of the *vanitas* topos. Painted in 1656, the painting, its light and chiaroscuro the influence of Caravaggio, is replete with symbols of death, the most striking of which is the huge dominant figure of a winged skeleton. The sad looking seated woman is probably allegorically present as Nyx (Roman: Nox) who in mythology is the goddess of night responsible for the dawn of creation. She sits on a fragile glass globe, dressed in white, somberly holding a child on her lap also dressed in white. The presence of two of Nyx's progeny – that's Thanatos who stands in the funeral urn ensuring his torch is lit, and Hypnos, standing in front of the urn, blowing effervescent bubbles – assures the woman's identity as Nyx. The goddess, however, was most commonly depicted with her twins on her lap. Who, then, is the child also clothed in white, who has usurped their place? The placid demeanor of the child she holds belies the dour *memento mori* message he is writing as winged skeletal Death hovers and guides his hand. Clearly readable on the parchment is a 12th century poem by Adam of St. Victor: *"Conception culpa, nasci pena, labor vita, necesse mori"* – "conceived in sin, birth a sorrow, life is hard, death inevitable."

Rosa's choice of an innocent toddler to convey the written *memento mori* message at first glance appears to be nothing more than an effective, ironic artistic device until one asks oneself why Rosa painted it. Now in the art and antiquities Fitzwilliam Museum of the University of Cambridge, the museum provides a detailed history of Rosa's inspiration for the work. In 1655, Rosa's son, Rosalvo, Rosa's brother, sister, husband and five of their children all died of the plague that had ravaged the city. A letter to a friend reveals the artist's grief: *"This time heaven has struck me in such a way that shows me that all human remedies are useless and the least pain I feel is when I tell you that I weep as I write."*[10] The symbolism in the painting with regards to the woman and child elicits pitiful sadness with the astonishing realization the figures are Rosa's beloved Lucrezia and their son who was taken from them so cruelly by the plague.

This heroic-sized allegorical reminder of the transience of life that incorporates every iconographic conceit of mortality used in 17th century Italian art in the painting is clearly more than at first meets the eye. Behind

"Nyx" is a bust of Terminus the god of Death, and at her feet are an array of death symbols – an owl, spent rockets, and a knife (with Rosa's initials on it). A memorial stele in the back-ground has reliefs of the Ages of Man, what is said to be a hippopotamus, representative of discord at the end of life and a fish (is it the only Christian emblem in the painting or, as contended by the Fitzwilliam Museum, a symbol of death and hatred?). The two butterflies at rest on the urn and the bubbles speak to the brevity of life; the faces of a child and on old man at the top of the painting refer to a normal life span. The falcon below, partially hidden by the skeleton's wing represents the vigor and energy of life denied Rosa's family. Knowing the personal story of the creator of *L'Umana Fragilita*, we leave this initially disturbing work haunted by the tragic beauty of its narrative. On a pleasant note, Lucrezia and Rosa had one more child, a son, who survived his artist father.

Fig. 181. Rosa. *Human Fragility* (1656).

187

Two large paintings intended as pendants, executed in 1670 by Spaniard Juan de Valdés Leal (1622-1690) – *In ictu oculi* (Fig. 182) and *Finis gloriae mundi* (Fig. 183) – are a mother lode pair of *vanitas* that simply startle. No pathos here. The title of one, *In ictu oculi* ("in the blink of an eye") provides immediate shock value. Skeletal death carries a coffin, shroud and scythe. With his right hand he extinguishes a candle in a *sic transit Gloria mundi* reference. He straddles the trappings of wealth and power with one foot on a globe and the other foot on a swatch of rich red satin, symbolic of church power. Before him are numerous symbols of learning and scholarship, crowns and tiaras (signifying power) all strewn about, and of course, useless, worthless, as Death holds sway.

The pendant, *Finis gloriae mundi* (another reference to the concept of "thus ends the glory of the world)," displays a vault full of decaying corpses. A bishop, emblem of the Church, a knight, symbol of military might and authority, and others of the body politic, are in varying stages of decomposition. The hand of God extends from a cloud above a *transi*, holding a set of scales. In one are the symbols of the seven deadly sins and, in the other, symbols of Christian faith that include charity, prayer and penance. The presence of an owl, placid and passive, is disconcerting, but not as much as knowing the two paintings were commissioned by the Hospital de la Caridad, in Seville and remain in view there for all of its pensioners and paupers to see.

Fig. 182. Leal. *In Ictu Oculi.*

188

Fig. 183. Leal. *Finis Gloria Mundi.*

The final example of this theme comes from the hand of Jacob Matham (1571-1631) in *Vanitas – Symbols of Death* (Fig. 184), a copper engraving produced in 1599. On one side of the work is Youth, with rich foliage and trees in the background. In the background on the opposite side, symbolizing things to come, is a small, bent and aging figure who carries a staff as support for his journey, and an ill-omened withered tree and fleeing birds. In the foreground of the engraving is the chilling icon of shrouded, skeletal Death, holding his lethal arrow. Multiple morality dictums surround the etching. Death symbols subtly occupy the corners of the work: in the left corner is a winged hourglass. On the right is a smoking vase and skull that rest on the ledge. Behind the skull, is another element of death iconography: the shadow of Death is projected on the pillar. An ancient theme, dating to the New Kingdom of Egypt (1570-1080 BCE), depicted the shadow of Death accompanying the soul (*ba*) leaving the body. During the Renaissance, the *Book of Psalms* 144:4 inspired the image: "Man is like to vanity, his days are as a shadow that passeth away," and the book of Job, 29:15 "Your life is as a shadow that will swiftly pass". An image of the adumbration of death was a powerful one that would have filled all with foreboding that death was nigh.

Fig. 184. Jacob Matham after Karel van Mander. *Symbols of Death.*

The iconography of death that evolved in the Christian world during the Middle Ages, Renaissance and Reformation, appeared as terrifying reminders and dire warnings of mortality. By the beginning of the 20th century they fell into disuse, and, today, only the dark hooded figure of Death carrying a scythe is generally recognized. "The Grim Reaper," as he is known, is no longer taken very seriously, and is more commonly the subject of dark humor in cartoons.

♣

Postclassical Child Funereal Iconography

Paintings

Four genre paintings appeared during the 16th century with iconography specific to the death of a child: the donor portrait, the epitaph painting, the family portrait and the solitary portrait. At first sight, most of these seem uncomplicated, but on close inspection unique iconography becomes apparent.

During the 1500s, the Renaissance tradition of donor painting became popular amongst the well-to-do who sought divine intervention and graces through the commission of a religious work for which they paid handsomely. The patron or donor was always included in the painting (see Figure 2). Initially, the donors were depicted as small homunculi since the religious subjects of paintings were the focal points. That was also true regarding depictions of children in such scenes. They were literally and figuratively little and insignificant. As religious subject matter was relegated to lesser levels of importance in paintings, donors and their families began to be larger, full scale figures. A Dutch innovation embellished this feature by including those members of the family who had died, as with the entire Cat family (Fig. 185) in Jacob van Oostanen's triptych, *The Adoration of the Magi*, painted in 1517. The central panel portrays the Adoration, and the family is grouped on the two wings of the triptych. The men are in the left panel*, father and six sons and his patron saint, Saint Jerome. Partially hidden, one of the children is wearing a grave-robe, an innovative device of the artist to indicate that he had died. On the right wing, the donor's wife with St. Catherine of Alexandria is depicted with her seven daughters, the smallest of whom had died. She too is partially hidden by the mother's right elbow and revealingly dressed in the grave-robe.

---

*In 16th and 17th century northern Europe, gender grouping became the model for family portraits in general.

Fig. 185. Jacob van Oostanen. *The Cat Family Triptych.*

Detail of Boys (AP)   Detail of Girls (AP)

Similarly, burial-clothing identifies the two dead sons in the lower left of the anonymous painting in 1560 of the Valckenier family. At the lower left are two dead sons and, next to them, a brother who holds a broken egg, symbolic of a lost child (perhaps as a newborn). In the lowlands and France, the wish extended to the mother was that the baby be "Wise as salt, good as bread, full as an egg, and straight as a match."[11] A broken egg came to mean a wasted life.

Fig. 186. Anon. *The Valckenier Family* (AP).

Detail, two deceased boys

The epitaph painting originated in Sweden. These were depictions commissioned to be placed in a church or altar niche, similar to the Meso and South American *retablo* popular during the Spanish-Baroque occupation of the New World. All epitaph paintings had four necessary characteristics: 1) the work was always a family portrait that included all children – dead and alive; 2) males were always one side of the central religious theme, females on the other, and both groups were positioned by descending age; 3) central to the work was a religious theme; 4) an epitaph always was included, usually somewhere near the religious theme. The epitaph generally expressed ideas of comportment and emphasized virtues. Most of these portraits were executed by itinerant painters who (like American limners) uncommonly signed their works. At the height of their popularity, in the mid-seventeenth century, they were being produced in almost all of Protestant Europe (without iconoclastic intent).

Fig. 187. Johan Dürch. *The Hjortberg Family* (c. 1760).

Of particular interest, is the manner in which dead children of the family were depicted to indicate they were deceased: pale to white complexions, partially hidden, backs to the viewer. At times the eyes were closed, or crosses appeared above their heads, or they held attributes of death in their hands. One example found in the Släp Church in Vallda, Sweden, is signed. It is a painting of the family of the Reverend Gustaf Fredrik Hjortberg by Johan Dürch (n.d.). This epitaph painting, complete with all the characteristics of the genre, additionally showcases the minister's great interest in natural science. To the viewer, the men are all on the left in chronological age order, and among them are three dead male children partially concealed among the four living members. The women, in similar fashion, are on the right. There are four girls depicted, two in cradles who had died. The iconographic conceit of partially obscuring a dead child is unique to the genre and the iconography of death in children.

Multiple births were rare occurrences, and more rarely did the infants survive. Several extraordinary extant paintings of multiple births exhibit iconography reserved for dead children. An anonymous Dutch work painted in 1621 depicts the quadruplets of Dordrecht (Fig. 188) born to Jacobis and Cornelia Pietersz: Pieter (five days old), Ianette and Maria (three days old). Elisabet (third born) lived only one and one-half hours. She was painted with a pale complexion and dressed in a white burial shroud wearing a wreath of rosemary which was believed to ward off demons for the non-baptized. In the painting, it appears Elisabet had a club-foot on her right leg, perhaps associated with other congenital defects. By 1622 only one of the quads was still alive. The other children may have died due to small gestational development, common to multiple births – or from one of the many common infections that at that time killed nearly 50% of children before the age of two years. The scroll cites Psalm 127 – "Children are a heritage from the Lord. Blessed is the man whose quiver is full of them...."

Fig. 188. Anon. *Dordrecht Quadruplets.*

Fig. 189. *De Wikkelkinderen.*

De Wikkelkinderen babies in arms (Fig. 189) in the Dutch castle, Muiderslot, are depicted swaddled in fine white linen with the family coat of arms visible above each child (1617). Both have eyes open, indicating they were live-born, but the twin on the right did not survive, evidenced by its pasty white complexion, whereas the twin on the left's complexion is normal. There are no pathophysiologic features to suggest that this was twin-transfusion syndrome.

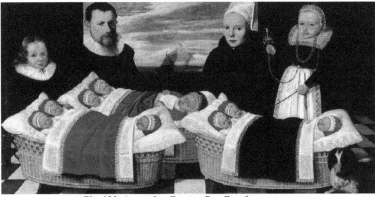

Fig. 190. Anon. *Jan Gerritsz.Pan Family.*

Another anonymous work depicts a family from Enkhuizen. The painting (Fig. 190), painted in 1638, has an inscription that indicates Jan Gerritsz.Pan was aged 32, and his wife, Wybrich, was 31 years of age. The boy next to the father was three years old, and the girl next to the mother, holding a teething coral cum rattle, was two. The composition, however, is dominated by three wicker cradles with a total of nine dead infants. Six have their eyes closed, an indication they were stillborn, and three have their eyes opened, suggesting that they were live-born and perhaps lived several days, even weeks. Conjecturally, they are said to have been three sets of triplets. It is known the couple had eight additional children – nineteen in all.

Some family portraits excluded the parents and focused on the children, depicting deceased siblings partially concealed in clouds, a reference that they were in heaven. A depiction by Jan Jansz.deStomme (1615-1657) of the children of Tjarda van Strachenborch in 1654 (Fig. 191), is an exemplum. The children are painted standing next to sixteen family coats of arms suspended by two ribbons. Frederica, who holds a stemmed orange, is five years old. The identities of the other two children are in question, although the small head in the clouds is believed to be son Lambert, who died before attaining the age of one year.

191. Jan Jansz.de Stomme. *Van Strachenborch Children.*

Johann Weidner (d. 1706) of Augsburg painted Carl Gustaf Göransson Ulfsparre in 1656 (Fig. 192). The child is depicted resplendently as an angel holding a sprig of green and wearing a wreath with an inscription overhead that reads simply "Victoria," thereby consigning his soul to heaven. He is dressed in classical robes, a 17th century motif commonly employed to portray dead children.

A child wearing a funereal head wreath (*hoedje* or "little hat"), whether painted as if alive or sleeping (Fig. 193), was always indicative of death. Postmortem portraits were a common memento òf well-to-families, just as in Victorian times, as we shall see, were photographs.

Fig. 192. Weidner. *Carl Gustaf Ulfsparre* (AP).

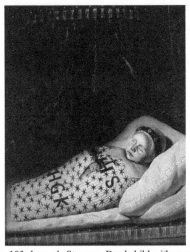

Fig. 193. Jansz.de Stomme. Dead child with wreath.

Some generalization can be made about deathbed portraits: almost always the identity of the limner is unknown, the subject is always laid out in finery with a headdress and holding a special token in their folded hands. Only well-to-do families commissioned such remembrances.

The Reformation had squarely placed the responsibility for religious training in the hands of the parents. The salvation of the soul and the rewards of Paradise for the child were the goals for all Christian parents. Thus, when a child died, the good parent imagined the child heaven-bound, virtually in God's grasp. The theme of the "Heaven-bound child" is best exemplified in the works of Nicholas Maes (1634-1693). Maes was often commissioned to paint dead children. One of his common conceits was to depict a male child as Ganymede heaven bound (Fig. 194). The mythology was that Zeus fell in love with the child Ganymede and, to the outrage of the cupbearer Hebe, Zeus came down in the form of an eagle to carry Ganymede off to Mount Olympus to serve there as the new cupbearer to the gods. The theme commonly is interpreted with homoerotic connotations,* but in the hands of Maes, it was a Neo-Platonic and Christian interpretation intended to console the parents, and as such, although a pagan theme, it was unopposed by Protestant parents who believed in predestination.

Fig. 194. Maes. *George de Vicq as Ganymede.*

*Starting around 630 BCE Greek poets assigned to the gods *eromenos*, an adolescent boy as a sexual companion.

199

Fig. 195.Thopas. *Girl on Deathbed.*

Single portraits of children in their deathbeds were common among the Dutch. Johannes Thopas (c.1620-c.1682) in 1682 painted a girl belonging to the van Valkenburg family (Fig. 195). She lies on a large, luxurious bed, dressed in a white bodice with puffed sleeves. In her white lace cap, she appears simply to be asleep. The device of a red curtain pushed aside for a viewing, however, is the clue that the still figure is dead. (Reference *Death of the Virgin* Fig. 91)

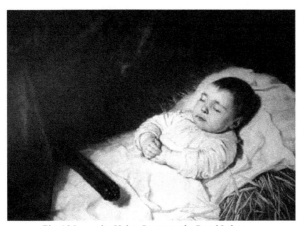

Fig. 196. van der Helst. *Portrait of a Dead Infant.*

Bartolomeus van der Helst (1613-1670) painted a dead infant in 1645 (Fig. 196). The identity of the child is unknown, but short hair and torch suggest it is a boy. Resting on his legs is the extinguished torch of life. He lies on a bed of straw, believed to prevent attachment of the soul to the bedding. The straw was burned after the burial.

A work that amalgamates epitaph and *lit de parade* depictions comes from Upper Swabia in the Church of St. Stephan. It shows Gottfried von Schwendi who died in 1566 (Fig. 197). Note the small hourglass next to the crucifix.

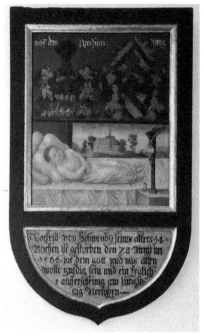

Fig. 197. Anon. *Gottfried von Schwendi.*

For the most part these Netherlandish death portraits and those of other northern European countries lacked psychic drama and were intentionally somewhat dispassionate. Although genuine grief may have prompted the commissions, the works were bereft of sentiment and more perceptibly expressed resolute stoicism. It was an age that accepted God's will and divine predestination. Clerics in fact suggested that parents not weep for a child who had joined God's kingdom.

Not all depictions of children in death were devoid of emotion. A work by Englishman William Dobson (1611-1646) is infused with emotive characteristics in each member of the family portrait (Fig. 198), painted around 1645. The Yale Center for British Art, Paul Mellon Collection believes they are probably Anne and Richard Streatfield and their children. Central to Dobson's painting is the father and mother. The father's stoic demeanor belies inner sorrow in a portrait that is rich with symbols of death: there are several skulls on the top of a broken pillar in the upper right corner and two sad looking small children on the left, one of whom proffers a cluster of cherries (fruit of paradise – mentioned in table 5) to a poised and dignified mother. Her face reveals a myriad of emotions. She is controlled and unwavering and appears sad but not sullen. Both she and her husband austerely appear resolved. However, she clutches a child to her side with one hand and with the other points a finger towards the child. It is the clue that the child had died, and we are left with the impression that all of the family are bereft. That gesture launched an inventive and original conceit regarding a deceased child in a portrait. Pointing figures in paintings had hitherto been common as an accusatory gesture or to emphasize an attribute of an individual. A banker, for example, pointed to the coins that made him rich; a lawyer, to scales of justice and a geographer, to a globe. In military commemorations, triumphant military leaders pointed to a victorious battlefield, or to command troops to engage in a battle. Here, the finger pointed at the child, who is arrayed in a Baroque garment in contrast to her parents' funereal black, is unique and contributes to the pervading sense of loss visible on the faces of all of the family members in contrast to the pleasant and engaging expression on the child lost to them. The pointed finger became part of artists' inventory of death iconography.

Fig. 198. William Dobson. *Portrait of a Family.*

202

The renowned Rococo/Neoclassical artist, Elizabeth Vigée le Brun (1755-1842) used the gesture and embellished on it in her magnificent portrait of Marie-Antoinette (1755-1793) and her children, painted in 1787 (Fig. 199). Often referred to as a propaganda painting to improve the detested queen's image with her people, indeed it was not customary to include children in a formal, monumental portrait of a resplendent monarch. Marie Antoinette's daughter, Marie Therese Charlotte languidly leans on her mother, and the queen looks straightforwardly with a passive, if not sad expression on her face. The dauphin, Louis, points to an empty cradle, by now a well known symbol the child had died. In this instance, the cradle, elegantly shrouded in funereal black, is a reference to the death of the queen's infant, Sophie-Béatrix, who had died as the portrait was being painted. This awareness completely alters one's reaction to the painting, diminishing the value of the impressive richness of the scene and the opulence of the velvets and silks of the apparel of the queen and her children. We are left with a sympathetic appreciation of a brave mother and children in mourning. Louis himself would die just a few years later, and the boy on the lap of the queen would become the second, hapless, dauphin who languished, miserably treated, in prison and died at the age of ten of tuberculosis after the assassination of his parents in 1793. Only the eldest child of Louis XVI and Marie Antoinette, Marie Therese Charlotte, imprisoned for more than three years, survived the excesses of the French Revolution. She lived to be seventy-two years old.

Fig. 199. Vigée le Brun. *Children of Marie Antoinette.*

Initially, in 1772, Charles Wilson Peale (1741-1827), at his wife's request, painted their daughter, Margaret, as she lay on her bed dead from smallpox. The iconographic chin strap that dates back to ancient times, the bound arms, her closed eyes and ashen skin tone did not detract from her artist father's intention to memorialize the child's beauty and innocence, and he skillfully preserved that memory with the sweet expression on the baby's face. Peale reworked and enlarged the painting as *Rachel Weeping** (Fig. 200) by 1776, in which the black background was erased from the original and the figure of his wife was painted, mourning at the child's bedside, eyes in supplication upward and tears on her cheek. It is an emotionally charged image that more profoundly reflects the anguish of both Peale and his wife that apparently never abated. Peale in 1818, 46 years after he first painted the image of his dead child, returned once more to his work for a retouching of the painting.

Fig. 200. Charles Wilson Peale. *Rachel Weeping.*

*Peale's title may have been inspired by biblical references to Rachel weeping.

The Graham Children was painted by William Hogarth (1697-1764) in 1742. It is a delightful painting of the children of King George II's apothecary, Daniel Graham. The children are gay, jaunty, playful and endearing. As seven year old Richard accompanies a song bird and nine year old Henrietta, dressed in blue, and five year old Anna Maria in a sprightly print, step in time, none notice their inquisitive cat leering at the caged bird, an insinuation of the piquant mischief of childhood. Two year old Thomas sits happily enjoying the frivolity. Reminders of the transience of life skillfully counterbalance the jovial mood the children evoke as Hogarth makes clear that the youngest child, Thomas had died (while, in fact, Hogarth was painting the portrait.) by inserting a scythe-bearing winged-putto on the mantel above Thomas' head.

Fig. 201. William Hogarth. *The Graham Children.*

By the end of the 18th century, the commemoration of children in paintings waned as, during the Victorian Age, silver gelatin photography was introduced. Besides being more economical – and portable – photography was instantaneous and gave true likenesses of a subject that conferred emotional power. It became possible, for the first time, for a tragic event etched forever in the minds of the bereaved to be preserved for all time.

Fig. 202. Dead Victorian child.

Sculpture

The material most suited to commemorative art throughout history has been stone, and, especially, marble, as we have seen when discussing the stelae and sarcophagi of memorials in the ancient world in which children were most typically depicted engaged as they had been in life. Postclassical representations illustrate how viewpoints and tastes shift and change with the times. Although there are only few Renaissance examples, there are a sufficient extant number of commemoratory tributes to suggest a sleeping child was the preferred statuary iconograph of death. Around 1490, wealthy Florentine widow Maria Pereira commissioned a tomb from Silvestro dell'Aquila (fl. 1471-1504). She wished her long departed 15-month-old daughter, Beatrice, to be commemorated with her. In the monument in San Bernadino, Aquila depicts both mother and daughter as if asleep, with the child, Beatrice, resting under her mother's gisant and sarcophagus.

Fig. 203. *Tomb of Maria Pereira.*

206

Following the Reformation, the image of sculpted children serenely asleep began to connote peaceful rest in the presence of God. Penelope Boothby died at the age of six years in 1793. Neoclassicist Thomas Banks (1735-1805) immortalized her dressed in an empire-style gown, her hands folded at her chin, lying on a buttoned-mattress, with her head resting on a folded pillow atop a sepulcher with strigillation and acroteria. The tomb, with a memorial inscription, is in a quiet niche of St. Oswald Church in Ashbourne in the United Kingdom.

Fig. 204. Thomas Banks. *Penelope Boothby.*

Strigillation is a design (see above) found in 3ʳᵈ and 4ᵗʰ century Roman sarcophagi. It is a distinct pattern that immediately places it in time and place, but the origins of the design are obscure. It is suggested that the repetitive shallow S-shaped pattern resembles rippling water and perhaps is a sign of crossing over the waters in death.

In 1817, Francis Chantrey (1781-1841) sculpted a memorial tomb called *The Sleeping Children* (Fig. 205). The work was commissioned by the mother, Ellen Robinson, to honor her daughters Ellen Jane and Marianne who had died in a fire. Chantrey used the death mask of one child to paint her likeness. He painted her sister with only familial features. The children lie together on a divan and appear to be asleep. In an affectionate embrace, the younger child has one arm around the neck of her sister and clutches snowdrops in the other arm that extends across her sister's torso. The exceptional realism of this beautiful tribute to the Robinson girls moves one to think a simple touch would reawaken them. Chantrey sculpted a few adults in a sleeping pose, but it was a conceit he mostly reserved for children. James Hamilton Stanhope, heartbroken by the death in childbirth of both his twenty-three year old wife, Frederica Louisa Stanhope and their infant – his namesake – commissioned Chantrey to sculpt a large memorial to honor them. *The Stanhope Monument* (Fig. 206) was completed in 1827. Part of the inscription on the tomb reads, "Her Life was all Purity and Happiness, Its Pious Close Like the Slumber of a Child." Chantrey's elegant sculpture poignantly portrays the mother and child, lying on their sides on a classical divan. The mother's graceful curves, the willowy drape of her gown and her beautiful young face lovingly gazes down at her infant who lies besides her, suckling, all enhance the sense of tragic loss the sculpture conveys.

Fig. 205. Francis Chantrey. *The Sleeping Children.*

Fig. 206. Francis Chantrey. *The Stanhope Monument.*

In 1859, a work by William Rinehart (1825-1874), was simply called *Sleeping Children* (208). It is in Greenmount Cemetery in Baltimore.

208

The children, no more than toddlers, rest on what appears to be a soft mattress and pillow in a gentle embrace. The marble divan is in the classical style. A memorial of the children of Hugh Sisson, the sculpture's theme was from a popular poem of the times by Lydia Sigourney (1791-1865): "Not dead but sleepeth ... There spoke a wishful tenderness – a doubt whether to grieve or sleep, which Innocence alone can wear." Rinehart's sculpture so appealed to Victorian romanticism, that he was commissioned to make at least twenty-five replicas in plaster and in marble.

Fig. 207. William Rinehart. *Sleeping Children* (1869) (AP).

By the end of the 19th century, memorial images of children in death were rare – in any medium. Sensibilities had changed, and stark reminders of child death, however realistic the commemorations, were no longer appealing. The few commissions that were sculpted, depicted a child at play, praying, engaged in an affectionate pose with a pet or family member, or, as in Figure 208, a casual likeness of the deceased in stone. Memorials for children became mostly epigrammatic and verbal sentiments, often sentimental, devoid of all classic iconography of millennia past such as have been written about in these pages.

We leave it up to you to discover meaningful iconography in the abstractions and installations of the contemporary art world. Have fun.

Fig. 208. Tomb of Child in St. Brélade cemetery, Island of Jersey.

Footnotes: Chapter Five

1. Patristic exegetists insisted all knowledge except theological was useless. Tertullian (160-220) said "For us curiosity is no longer necessary." Added Ambrose (340-397) "To discuss the nature and position of the earth does not help us in our hope of the life to come."

2. Dionysian and Bacchant themes were favorites, depicted as celebratory symposiums in which the soul was expected to triumphantly march through the underworld, reaching the promise of eternal felicity.

3. Lucian, *Charon, or the Inspectors* (London: Heinemann, 1924) 16.

4. Jonathan Tubb, Ancient Levant curator, British Museum. Personal communication.

5. The theme of Eros-Thanatos has roots in antiquity, Greek myths that give emphasis to the sacrificial aspects of love. These stories revolve around lovers attempting to unite, stories that end in tragedy. Examples are those of Orpheus and Eurydice and Pyramus and Thisbe, both immortalized in Ovid's *Metamorphoses.* Renaissance artisans and patrons held a fascination with these stories and with Love and Death as themes for prose and painting. Petrarch's Laura and *Trionfo della Morte* and the *Decameron* of Boccaccio – fueled by the apocalyptic Black Plague – are examples in poetry and prose of this preoccupation with neo-platonic or courtly love. The lofty cult of Courtly Love, however, was, at the same time, marred by the reality and horror of the pestilence. In its place began to appear prose that suggested death and physical pleasure – Love – are at opposite poles of the same continuum. Love was often blamed as causes of tragedy, especially Death – and Death was thought to immortalize Love. To the favorite themes of Orpheus and Eurydice and Pyramus and Thisbe, were added Tristan and Isolde. The arrow attribute of Eros was now also to be found in the hands of Thanatos. The popular and unfathomable fantasy-erotic novel, the *Hypnerotomachia Poliphili* (1499) of Dominican priest Francesco Colonna (1433-1527) thrust Courtly Love into the dream world where Hypnos and Thanatos lived. The etymology of the title – *hypnos* (sleep), *eros* (love) and *mache* (strife) of Poliphilus– reflects the conflict.

6. There is conflict of attribution. Some scholars believe the legend is 13th century French by Baudoin de Condé; others attribute the work to a 15th

century middle English *MS Douce 302* by a Shropsire clergyman John Audelay. The quotation here is from the French.

7. Sobel, Dava. *Galileo's Daughter*. New York: Penguin, 2000.

8. Lucian, *Charon, or the Inspectors* (London: Heinemann, 1924) 16.

9.   "Quadratum infoditus firmissima tessera saxum,
       Stat cirrata super pectore imago tenus.
       Et sese nullis profitetus cedere. Talis
       Terminus est, homines qui scopus unus agit.
       Est immota dies, praefixaque tempora fatis,
       Deque ferunt primis ultima judicium."

       Andrea Alciati, *Emblematum Liber, 1531*. No. 157.

10. Comments and quotations about the painting derive from the extensive research and analysis of the Fitzwilliams Museum of Cambridge University which can be accessed through their website.

11. Sage comme le sal, bon comme le pain, plein come oeuf, et droit come allumette.

BIBLIOGRAPHY

Alciati, Andrea. *Emblemata Lyon* (1550). Trans. B. Knott. New York: Scholar Press, 1996.

Amt, E. *Women's Lives in Medieval Europe.* New York: Routledge, 1993.

Aries, Philippe. *The Hour of Our Death.* New York: Knopf, 1981.

-----------. *Centuries of Childhood.* New York: Vintage, 1965.

-----------. *Images of Man and Death.* Boston: Harvard UP, 1985.

Baptist, Jan and Rudi Ekkart. *Pride and Joy: Children's Portraits in the Netherlands 1500-1700.* Amsterdam: Ludion, 2001.

Barolsky, Paul. "The Genitals of Jesus in Perspective." *Source.* 26(1): 34-36, 2006.

Battistini, Matilde. *Symbols and Allegories in Art.* (Trans Stephen Sartarelli). Los Angeles: Getty Museum, 2005.

Bedard, Emily. "Pygmalion and Galatea," *Art History Journey.* Sept, 2006. Lyme Academy, Old Lyme, CT.

Bellosi, Luciano. "Buffalmacco." *Dictionary of Art.* Ed. Jane Turner. New York: Grove, 1996. Vol. 5, pp. 123-124.

Bedaux, Bialostocki, Jan. *The Message of Images.* Vienna: Irsa, 1988.

Biedermann, Hans. *Dictionary of Symbolism.* Trans. J. Hulbert. New York: Meridian, 1992.

Blunt, Anthony. *Picasso's Guernica.* New York: Oxford UP, 1979.

Bullfinch, Thomas. *The Age of Fables* (1834). New York: Harper, 1970.

Burn, Barbara. *Metropolitan Children.* New York: Abrams, 1984.

Buxton, Richard. *The Complete World of Mythology.* London: Thames & Hudson, 2004.

Cahill, Thomas. *Mysteries of the Middle Ages.* New York: Doubleday, 2006. pp. 44-50.

Caldwell, Richard. *Hesiod's Theogony.* Focus Information Group, 1987.

Castiglioni, Arturo. *A History of Medicine.* New York: Knopf, 1958.

Cavalli-Björkman, Görel. *Face to Face.* Stockholm: National Museum, 2001.

Cheney, Liana. "Love and Death." *Encyclopedia of Comparative Iconography.* Ed. Helene Robert. Chicago: Fitzroy, 1998. Vol. I., pp. 521-526.

Chu, Petra. "Sleep/Sleeping." *Encyclopedia of Comparative Iconography.* Ed. Helene Robert. Chicago: Fitzroy, 1998. Vol. II., pp. 845-850.

Colón, Angel Rafael and Patricia Ann Colón. *A History of Children.* Westport: Greenwood, 2001.

-----------. *Tincture of Time: A Concise History of Medicine.* Charleston: Amazon, 2011.

Colonna, Francesco. *Hypnerotomachia Poliphili* (1499). Trans. Jocelyn Godwin. London: Thames, 1999.

Corcoran, James. *The Triumph of Death.* Antwerp: Museum Mayer van den Bergh, 1993.

Craske, Matthew. *Art in Europe 1700-1830.* Oxford: Oxford UP, 1997.

de Jongh, Eddy. *Question of Meaning: Theme and Motif in Dutch Seventeenth-Century Painting.* Trans. Michael Hoyle. Leiden: Primavera, 2000.

de Vos, Dirk. *Hans Memling.* Antwerp: Ludion, 1994.

Diesner, H.J. *The Great Migration.* Leipzig: Hippocrene, 1978.

Durantini, Mary Frances. *The Child in Seventeenth-Century Dutch Painting.* Ann Arbor: UMI Research, 1983.

Eberly Jr, John Brewer. "Look. Listen. Receive." *JAMA* 317: 1508, 2017.

Evans, J.K. *War, Women, and Children in Ancient Rome.* London: Routledge, 1991.

Ferguson, George. *Signs and Symbols in Christian Art*. Oxford: Oxford UP, 1961.

Field, Richard S. *Images of Death*. Middletown: Wesleyan UP, 1975.

Forty, Sandra. *The World of Art*. London: PRC Publishing, 1998.

Garland, Robert. *The Greek Way of Life*. Ithaca: Cornell University Press, 1990.

Godfrey, E. *English Children in Olden Times*. New York: Dutton, 1907.

Golden, M. *Childhood in Classical Athens*. Baltimore: John Hopkins UP, 1990.

Goodich, Michael. Rev. of *"The Black Death,"* by Ole Benedictow. *Speculum* 81.1 (2006): 146-147.

Graham-Dixon, Andrew. *Renaissance*. London: BBC Worldwide, 1999.

Grossman, Janet. *Greek Funerary Sculptures*. Los Angeles: Getty Museum, 2001.

Hall, James. *Illustrated Dictionary of Symbols*. New York: Harper, 1994.

Hansen, Julie. "Resurrecting Death: Anatomical Art in the Cabinet of Dr. Fredrik Ruysch." *The Art Bulletin*. 78.4 (1996): 663-679.

Hartt, Frederick. *Michelangelo*. New York: Abrams, 1965.

Herlihy, D. *Medieval Households*. Cambridge: Harvard UP, 1985.

------------. "Medieval Children." *Walter Prescott Webb Memorial Lectures*. Austin: U of Texas P, 1978.

Holbein, Hans. *Holbeni Pictoris Alphabetum Mortis des Maer Hans Holbein*. Köln: J.M. Heberle, 1849.

Holy Bible (KJV). New York: Ottenheimer, 1994.

Horace. *Odes and Epodes*. Trans. T.E. Page. London: Loeb, 1914.

Horapollo. *The Heiroglyphica*. Trans. George Boas. New York: Bollingen Series XXIII. Pantheon, 1950.

Hughes, Robert. *The Shock of the New*. London: Thames and Hudson, 1991.

Huskinson, Janet. *Roman Children's Sarcophagi*. Oxford: Clarendon Press, 1996.

Jones, John. "Observations on the Origin of the Division of Man's Life into Stages." *Archaeologia*. 35 (1853): 167-189.

Jung, Carl. *Man and His Symbols*. New York: Doubleday, 1964.

Kelle, Kenneth D. *Leonardo da Vinci's Elements of the Science of Man*. New York: Academic Press, 1983.

Ken, Arnold. *Doctor Death: Medicine at the End of Life*. London: Wellcome, 1997.

Knipping, John B. *Iconography of the Counter Reformation in the Netherlands*. Leiden: Sijthoff, 1974.

Laupicher, Fritz. "Pointing/Indicating." *Encyclopedia of Comparative Iconography*. Ed. Helene Robert. Chicago: Fitzroy, 1998. Vol. II., pp. 739-744.

Lamia, Stephen. "Funeral/Burial." *Encyclopedia of Comparative Iconography*. Ed. Helene Robert. Chicago: Fitzroy, 1998. Vol. I., pp. 347-355.

Llewellyn, Nigel. *The Art of Death*. London: Reaktion, 1991.

Lover, Samuel. *Poetical Works*. New York: Sadlier, 1869.

Lucian. *Charon, or the Inspectors*. Trans. A.M. Harman. London: Heinemann, 1924.

-----------. *Dialogue of the Dead*. Trans. A.M. Harman. London: Heinemann, 1924.

Macho, Thomas. *Bilder vom Tod*. Vienna: Agens-Werk Geyer, 1992.

Male, Emile. *Religious Art in France*. Princeton: Princeton UP, 1986.

Martial. *Epigrams*. Trans. Walter Ker. London: Heinemann, 1933.

Musacchio, J. Marie. *The Art and Ritual of Childbirth in Renaissance Italy.* New Haven: Yale UP, 1999.

Neils, Jenifer and John H. Oakley. *Coming of Age in Ancient Greece.* New Haven: Yale UP, 2003.

Nuland, Sherwin B. *Leonardo da Vinci.* New York: Penguin Group, 2000.

Olds, Clifton C. and Ralph G. Williams. *Images of Love and Death in Late Medieval and Renaissance Art.* Ann Arbor: U of Michigan Museum of Art, 1975.

Orme, Nicholas. "The Dead Beneath our Feet." *History Today.* 54.2 (2004): 19-25.

Orozco, Sebastián. *Emblemas Morales* (1610). New York: Scolar, 1973.

Ozment, Steven. *When Fathers Ruled.* Cambridge: Harvard UP, 1983.

Panofsky, Erwin. *Studies in Iconography.* Boulder: Westview, 1973.

-----------. *Tomb Sculpture.* New York: Abrams, 1964.

Park, Katherine. "The Life of the Corpse." *Journal of the History of Medicine.* 50 (1995): 11-132.

Penny, Nicholas. *Church Monuments in Romantic England.* New York: Yale UP, 1977.

Quintilian. *Institutio Oratoria.*Vol. II. Trans. H.E. Butler. London: Heinemann, 1921.

Rawson, B. *Marriage, Divorce, and Children in Ancient Rome.* Oxford: Oxford U, 1991.

Read, Benedict. *Victorian Sculpture.* New Haven: Yale UP, 1982.

Ripa, Cesare. *Iconologia: Padua* (1611). New York: Garland, 1976.

Scaramella, P., A. Tenenti, M.G. Aurigemma, et. al. *Humana Fragilitas: I Temi della Morte in Europa tra Duecento e Settecento.* Clusone: Ferrari Grafiche, 2000.

Schaller, Wendy. *Children Borne Aloft: Nicolaes Maes's Ganymede Portraiture and the Context of Death and Mourning in the Seventeen-Century Netherlands.* Dissertation, Ohio State University, 2001.

Schama, Simon. *An Embarrassment of Riches.* New York: Alfred Knopf, 1987.

Schleif, Corine. "The Proper Attitude Towards Death." *The Art Bulletin.* 64 (1987): 587-603.

Scott, Jonathan. *Salvatore Rosa: His Life and Times.* New Haven: Yale UP, 1995.

Sears, Elizabeth. *The Ages of Man.* Princeton: Princeton UP, 1986.

Shakespeare, William. *Macbeth.* New Haven: Yale UP, 1918.

Sigourney, Lydia. *Pocahontas and Other Poems.* New York: Harper, 1841.

Smart, Alastair. *The Renaissance and Mannerism in Italy.* London: Thames and Hudson, 1971.

Sobel, Dava. *Galileo's Daughter.* New York: Penguin, 2000.
--------------. *The Planets.* New York: Viking, 2005.

Sommerville, C. John. *The Rise and Fall of Childhood.* New York: Vintage, 1990.

Stebbins, Theodore. *The Lure of Italy.* New York: Abrams, 1992.

Steinberg, Leo. *The Sexuality of Christ in Renaissance Art and in Modern Oblivion.* New York: Pantheon, 1983.

Thomas, Julia. *Victorian Narrative Painting.* London: Tate, 2000.

Vermeule, Emily. *Aspects of Death in Early Greek Art and Poetry.* Berkeley: UP California, 1979.

Wiedemann, T. *Adults and Children in the Roman Empire.* London: Routledge, 1989.

INDEX

220

Authors

Angel Rafael Colón is professor emeritus and adjunct professor to the dean at Georgetown University in Washington, DC, where he lectures on the history and philosophy of western medicine, the history of childhood, art iconography and clinical medicine. He holds graduate degrees in science, medicine, humanities/art history, and is boarded in medicine, pediatrics, gastroenterology and nutrition. A member of the Medieval Society and the American Association for the History of Medicine, he has over 175 publications, including ten books, of which four were written in collaboration with Patricia Ann Colón, among them *Nurturing Children: A History of Pediatrics* (Westport: Green-wood, 1999), *A History of Children: A Socio-Cultural Survey Across Millennia* (Westport: Greenwood, 2001) and *Tincture of Time: A Concise History of Medicine* (Charleston: Amazon.com. Fourth edition 2017).

Patricia Ann Colón is a free-lance writer with a graduate degree in English literature. She has served as a member of the Board of Directors of several health foundations and schools and on health related university committees. As cited above, this book is the fourth she has co-authored with ARC. Additionally, she has published articles on health and children in our society and in space! She has visited virtually every major and regional art museum worldwide to study their collections. She is currently finishing a novel, with a second on a back burner soon to be seasoned and sizzled, preferably whilst living in a seaside cottage in Ireland.

SAINT	SYMBOL - CONCEIT	ORIGIN
Agatha of Sicily	breast on plate, shears	Virgin whose breasts were hacked off before being burning at the stake
Agnes	lamb	Agnes, similar to the Latin, *agnus*, for lamb was adopted as her conceit
Alfred the Great	crown, scepter	The symbols are royal conceits, and this Wessex king kept England Catholic
Ambrose	bees, beehive, dove	In infancy, bees settled on his face, foretelling his gift of sweet eloquence
Andrew	saltire (x-cross)	One of the apostles, crucified on a saltire - x shaped cross
Anne, of Mary	open book	The maternal Anne, who taught Mary to read scripture
Ansgar	bishop, church model	In 845, Danes invaded Hamburg and Ansgar rebuilt the destroyed cathedral
Anthony the Great	pig, hood, T-staff	Monk who carried a tau -staff symbolizing the cross. Resisted gluttony (pig)
Anthony of Padua	lily, child Jesus	Lily = purity, Anthony had mystic visions of baby Jesus during prayer
Apollonia	tooth and tongs	Martyr who first had all her teeth pulled before being burned to death
Athanasius	book between pillars	A learned Alexandrian bishop of canon law
Augustine of Hippo	bishop, child, seashell	A bishop who equated understanding the Trinity with image of a child filling a seashore hole with a shell
Barbara	tower, chalice	Locked in tower because of her faith, requested sacramental wine before death
Barnabas	staff	Missionary who traveled widely carrying a staff and preaching the gospels
Benedict	broken cup, raven	Poisoned wine leaked from a crack; plagued by a raven of temptation
Benno of Meissen	fish, keys in mouth	To bar entry of Henry IV, cathedral keys thrown into Elbe and found inside a fish
Bernard of Clairvaux	drops of milk, bees	Had visions of lactating Mary; bees represent good order and work
Bernardino of Siena	sun with IHS, three miters	IHS - his devotion to Jesus; three bishoprics he refused
Blaise	iron carding combs, ax	Instruments of torture used to flay his skin; beheaded.
Bonaventure	ciborium, cardinal's hat	Both part of his coat of arms

Name	Attributes	Description
Boniface	oak, axe, sword	Cut down a giant oak pagans worshiped as the sanctuary of Thor
Bridget of Sweden	book, pilgrim staff	Abbess who traveled widely with a staff, preached, gave away books of meditation
Brigid of Kildare	Brigid's cross	Cross woven of reeds
Casimir of Poland	royal robe with ermine	Polish prince known for his devotion to Mary
Catherine of Alexandria	torture wheel	Instrument of her torture
Catherine of Ricci	coral ring	Mystically married to Christ with coral ring
Catherine of Siena	stigmata, Dominican habit	Nun who, after prayers, had wounds corresponding to those of Christ on the Cross
Cecilia	organ, harp, viola	Saint of music, who heard the songs of the angels and sang to God
Cerbonius	geese	Tamed wild geese with blessings and the sign of the Cross
Charles Borromeo	cardinal robe	Cardinal and leading figure of counter-reformation
Christopher	infant Jesus, staff	Patron saint of travelers, shown with staff & carrying Jesus
Claire of Assisi	monstrance, gray tunic	Wore the gray Franciscan habit and worshipped the Eucharist
Clement	anchor, fish,	Martyred by wearing an anchor and thrown into sea
Corbinian	saddled bear	When a bear killed his pack horse, he saddled the bear and rode him to Rome
Cosmas-Damian	transplanted leg, phial	Twin physicians who transplanted the leg of a Moor to a Christian; doctors to the poor
Crispin-Crispinian	shoes, millstone	Shoemaker twins, preached and made shoes at night; thrown into the river with millstones
Daniel	lion	Thrown into a den of lions, the animals did not attack him.
David of Scotland	king with sword	Catholic king who assumed the Scottish throne in 1124.
David of Wales	leeks and daffodils	Welsh bishop. Leeks and daffodils are symbols of Wales
Denis	head in hands	Martyred bishop of Paris, decapitated (see chapter one of text)
Dominic	rosary, dog with a torch	Rosary-devotion to Mary. Barren mother's dream of a dog with torch rendered her fertile
Donatus	broken cup	Bishop of Arezzo. A heathen broke a chalice during Mass, yet not a drop of wine was spilled
Dorothea of Caesarea	flowers, fruit	Martyr - sent 3 apples and 3 roses from heaven in reply to a taunt as she walked to martyrdom
Dunstan	hammer, tongs	A metalsmith in Glastonbury before becoming a monk and bishop; restored monasticism

Dymphna	crown, sword, lilies	Chaste Irish princess martyred by sword wielded by her mad, lusting father. Lilies = purity
Edmund martyr	arrow quiver	King of England shot with arrows, then beheaded
Edward confessor	king with nimbus, ring	Last Saxon king of England who built Norman style Westminster Abbey
Eligius	holding a church, hammer	English Bishop who was a skillful metalsmith, engraver; built the cathedral of St. Paul
Elijah	cave	Old Testament 1 Kings 19 describes how he lodged in a cave
Elizabeth of Hungary	alms, bread	Hungarian princess who served the poor with food and alms
Elizabeth of Aragona	crown	Spanish princess who served the poor
Erasmus	windlass	Italian bishop martyred by his intestines wrapped around a windlass
Euphemia	lion, wheel	Tortured on a wheel; thrown to lions that only licked her wounds. (finally killed by a bear)
Eustace (aka Placidus)	hunter, stag	Roman general who, while hunting, saw a cross on stag horns and was converted
Faith	brazier irons	Third century French maiden tortured with brazier irons
Felix	spider web	Persecuted 3rd century presbyter hid behind a door over which a spider spun a web
Fina	rat	Made garments for the poor until totally paralyzed, whereupon rats fed on her body
Florinus	glass of wine	Swiss Confessor said to have turned water into wine
Francis of Assisi	wolf, birds, stigmata	Patron of animals, stigmata appeared on his body during meditation
Francis Xavier	crucifix, crab with a cross	Spanish saint. Losing his cross in the sea, it was found when a netted crab held the cross
Gabriel	archangel, trumpet	God's messenger who heralds with a trumpet
Genesius	theater mask	Comic actor who, while performing for Diocletian,* experienced a vision and converted
Genevieve	bread	Gave bread to the poor; said to have saved Paris from Attila the Hun through prayer
George	dragon, knight, white horse	Roman soldier from Syria and a convert; killed a dragon that menaced a village's population
Giles	arrow and deer	Greek hermit who survived by drinking deer milk; martyred by an arrow
Gregory	papal tiara, dove at ear	Pope to whom the Holy Spirit in the form of a dove whispered wisdom to him

Name	Symbol	Description
Helena (Eleanor)	white crown with cross	Mother of Constantine said to have found the true cross on which Christ was crucified
Hippolytus	papal tiara, horse	Challenged popes (tiara) for their laxity, martyred by horse quartering
Honoratus of Amiens	baker's peel	Named a bishop, a bakers peel planted into ground, grew into mulberry bush
Hugh of Lincoln	swan	Bishop, best-known English saint after Thomas Becket, had pet sawn that followed him
Ignatius of Antioch	chained bishop and lion	Martyred in the Roman coliseum
Ignatius of Loyola	chasuble, letters AMDG	Priest and co-founder of Jesuits whose motto was AMDG
Irene of Thessalonica	palm frond	Persian princess martyred when she became a Christian
Isaac Jogues	native American	Jesuit missionary and martyr, served Iroquois and Huron tribes, martyred by Mohawks
Isidore of Seville	bishop attire, book, pen	Church father, garbed as a bishop and holding a pen and book
Ivo of Kermartin,	lawyer, document in hand	Ecclesiastical judge and advocate of the poor and children
James son of Zebedee	staff, scallop shell	Preached in Compostela, pilgrims to his shrine carry staff and wear a scallop shell
James son of Alphaeus	club	One of the twelve apostles, clubbed to death
Jerome	lion, cardinal dress, stone, books	(see text, pg. 4)
Joachim	doves in a basket	Father of Mary, made offerings in the temple
Joan of Arc	shield, knight,	Lorraine maiden; patroness of soldiers and France
Joanna	lamb	Healed by Jesus, became a follower of the Lamb of God
John the Baptist	lamb, animal skin, staff banner	Lived in wilderness (animal skin), proclaimed the Lamb of God with staff banner
John Berchmans	cross and rosary	Jesuit 'soldier of Christ' who had great devotion for the rosary
John Chrysostom	bees, pen	Early father of the church(pen), golden gift of preaching (bees)
John Nepomuk	silence-finger to mouth	Would not betray the secrecy of the confessional. Martyred by drowning
John the Evangelist	eagle, chalice with snake, book	Given poisoned wine, John blessed it, and the venom came out in the form of a snake
Joseph	lily, carpenter	Father of Jesus, a carpenter, pure of heart (lily)

Name	Symbol	Description
Jude	halberd	Apostle of Christ martyred by lance
Justin martyr	axe, sword	Second century Christian apologist martyred by a sword
Kevin of Glendalough	blackbird	While in a meditative trance, a blackbird built a nest in his hand
Knut IV of Denmark	Nordic king, lance	Devotedly supported Catholicism, martyred by a lance to his flank by rebels
Lambert	palm frond	Seventh century bishop of Maestricht, martyred at the altar. Palm frond sign of martyrdom
Lawrence	gridiron	Gave church wealth to the poor and was punished by superior by being grilled to death
Leander	pen	A church writer, and brother of Isidore of Seville
Leo the great	papal tiara	Fifth century pope who negotiated the withdrawal of Attila the Hun from Rome
Leonard	lock, fetters	Fifth century Frankish noble who released prisoners
Louis IX of France	golden fleur-de-lis	Symbol of French kings, he took active part in 7th and 8th crusades
Lucy	eyes on plate, lamp	Blinded because of her beauty. Parable of the wise virgin whose lamp is well lit
Luke	winged ox, palette	Painter and evangelist who emphasized the priesthood of Christ and sacrifice (winged ox)
Margaret of Scotland	reading book	Also known as Margaret of Wessex who spent much time in devotional reading
Margaret the virgin	dragon in chains	Of Antioch who subdued Satan as a dragon, keeping him under her feet with chains
Mark	winged lion, book	Evangelist (book). Winged lion represents Christ as the Lion of Judah
Martha	ladle, aspergillum	Home-maker (ladle). Defended herself from the dragon of temptation with holy water
Martin of Tours	goose, cloak to beggar	Gave half of his cloak to a beggar. To escape elevation to bishop he hid in a goose pen
Martin of Porres	broom, cat-dog-mouse	House servant (broom); cared for the sick, loved and fed all manner of creatures
Mary of Egypt	old woman, bread, lion	Prostitute, who repented and went into desert with 3 loaves of bread, a lion dug her grave
Mary Magdalen	jar of ointment, flowing hair	Washed the feet of Jesus, anointed them and dried them with her long hair
Matilda	purse, alms	Ninth century Westphalia queen known for giving alms to the poor
Matthew	winged man, purse	Tax collector (purse), biblical meanings of wings spiritual guidance and love

Name	Symbol	Description
Maurice	armor, banner with red cross	Roman soldier from Thebes who refused to kill Christians
Menas of Crete	two camels	The animals that returned his body to Egypt after martyrdom.
Michael	archangel, scales, dragon	Archangel who weighs souls at the Last Judgment, often depicted slaying a dragon
Monica of Hippo	nun's outfit	Mother of St. Augustine who became a nun
Mungo	fish with ring in mouth	Queen falsely accused of infidelity, catching a fish in which was her wedding band†
Nicholas of Bari	bishop, 3 gold balls, children	The Bishop provided dowry for poor women with gold, saved children in a barrel‡
Nicholas of Tolentino	black habit, star	Meteor flashed at his birth (star painted on his breast across black Augustinian habit)
Oda of Scotland	magpie in hand	Magpies directed her to a clearing where she built a convent
Olaf II of Norway	axe in coat of arms	Norway's Coat of Arms. Olaf, sought to Christianize all of Norway
Onuphrius	unkempt, wearing leaves, lions	Onofre from Thebes lived in the desert; two lions buried him
Pancras	sword	At age 14, beheaded in 304 during Diocletian's persecution
Pantaleon	nailed hands	Physician who defied Diocletian, tortured by hands nailed, then beheaded
Patrick	cross, harp, shamrock	Converted the Irish, Celtic cross, Irish harp, shamrock – 3 in 1 – explained the Trinity
Paul the Apostle	green robe, red mantle, horse	Costume worn by Saul when thrown from his horse
Paul the Hermit	raven, bread, old man	For over 90 years lived in the desert where a raven daily delivered bread
Peter the Apostle	gold and silver keys	Successor as head of Christ's church represented by keys to the kingdom given to him by Chri
Peter of Verona	Dominican, hatchet in head	How he was assassinated by Cathars in 1262
Petronius	bishop, model of Bologna	Roman noble who converted, entered priesthood and became bishop of Bologna
Philip the Apostle	cross, basket of bread	Apostle, crucified upside down. Fed five thousand bread – John 6:7, loaves and fish
Philip Neri	lily	Lily symbolized his chastity and his fatherly love
Philomena	anchor, arrow	Survived being thrown into the sea with an anchor. Shot with an arrow, and then decapitated

Saint	Symbols	Description
Quentin	spits anchored to chair	Manacled to a chair and tortured with a roasting a spit and beheaded.
Raphael	archangel, fish	With Tobias, used fish innards to cure father's blindness
Remigius	baptismal font	Bishop of Rheims who baptized the Frankish king Clovis
Reparata	dove from the mouth	Florentine martyred at age 12, as she died her soul was seen rising as a dove to heaven
Richard of Chichester	bishop with spilt chalice	Celebrating mass the chalice fell over but no wine was spilt
Rita	roses, thorns, stigma	Praying before the cross, a thorny stigmata appeared on forehead. In winter, her roses bloome
Robert Bellarmine	cardinal with IHS	Jesuit with IHS monogram, active in the counter-Reformation, Doctor of the Church
Roch	leg bubo, dog, pilgrim	Cared for plague victims; survived plague after a dog licked the buboes, mendicant pilgrim
Romuald	ladder to heaven	Founded an ascetic order with white habits based on a dream of men in white on a ladder
Rose of Lima	crown of thorns, anchor	Steadfast in belief (anchor); she wore a silver crown of thorns
Scholastica	lily, crucifix, dove	Devout nun, sister of St. Benedict. Lily – purity; dreamed her dove-soul ascended to heaven
Sebastian	arrows	Martyred with arrows by emperor Diocletian's men
Simon the Apostle	saw, boat, fish	Fisherman. Saw is the weapon of his martyrdom
Stephen	stones	Martyred by stoning
Stephen of Hungary	royal dress, double cross	King whose signature incorporates two crosses
Sylvester	bull lying at his feet	Restored a dead bull to life to prove Christ was the God of life
Teresa of Avila	heart, arrow, book	Carmelite writer whose heart was pierced by arrow in mystic marriage with Christ
Teresa of Lisieux	roses entwined around cross	French Carmelite 'After my death, I will let fall a shower of roses'
Theodore of Amasea	crocodile battle armor	Roman soldier and convert who defeated a dragon (crocodile) placed in his sanctuary
Thomas the Apostle	hand in Christ's wound	Thomas would not believe it was the resurrected Christ until he touched his wound
Thomas Aquinas	ox, Summa	Doctor of the Church, author of Summa Theologica. his nickname was "Ox"
Thomas Becket	neck chain, sword	Chain of office of archbishop of Canterbury, Henry II's knights killed him with swords
Thomas More	axe	Beheaded by Henry VIII for refusing to recognize divorce from Catherine Aragona

Name	Symbol	Description
Urban of Langres	bishop with grapes	While hidden from persecutors in a vineyard, he converted the vineyard keepers
Ursula	arrow, nuns	She and her fellow nuns were martyred by arrows
Vedast	wolf with goose, bear	Saved goose owned by a poor family from the mouth of a wolf
Verdiana	snakes	Lived in a small hermitage with two snakes as companions
Veronica	image of Christ on cloth	Met Christ on a journey and wiped sweat from his brow. His face appeared on the cloth
Victor of Marseilles	windmill	Roman soldier who would not worship Jupiter, crushed under a millstone
Vigilius of Trent	shoes or clogs	Destroyed a pagan statue and vengefully killed by a hail of clogs
Vincent de Paul	children	Depicted surrounded by devotion to child care
Vincent Ferrer	pulpit, trumpet	Eloquent preacher of the Apocalypse, represented by a trumpet
Vitus	rooster, caldron	Martyred in boiling in oil with a rooster
Wenceslaus	crown, dagger	AKA Václav the Good. After assassination by dagger, posthumously crowned king
William of Montevergine	wolf, pastoral staff	Having killed his donkey the saint turned the wolf into a beast of burden. Pastoral care
William of York	bishop crossing river	While crossing the river Ouse, the bridge collapsed and he suffered no injuries
Wolfgang	church with adze	Legend that he charmed the devil who helped him build a church
Xenia of Petersburg	walking stick	After her husband's death, she walked the streets of St. Petersburg helping the poor
Zachary	olive branch, dove	Eighth century pope who made peace with King Liutprand of Lombard and released prisoners
Zeno	fish hanging on crosier	Fisherman who became bishop of Verona, venerated for his kindness and generosity
Zenobius	flowering tree, rising the dead	Awoke the dead and a dead tree that thereafter bloomed every spring
Zita	bag, keys	Household servant who served the poor and found lost house keys. Patron of lost keys

233

*Diocletian, a Roman emperor from 284 to 305 initiated the Great Persecution of Christians in 303. Thus he appears frequently in this table with the martyred.

†The Mungo symbol refers to the story about a Queen suspected of infidelity by her husband. The King demanded to see her wedding band, which he claimed she had given to her lover, but actually the King had thrown it into the river. The Queen asked Mungo for help who ordered a fish caught from the river. On opening the fish, the ring was found inside, and the Queen was declared innocent.

‡Children in a barrel? This needs more explanation. St. Nicholas was considered a patron saint of child scholars based on a legend of two boys who went to Athens for study. They had been asked to present themselves to Bishop Nicholas upon arrival, but they postponed their visit, choosing instead to check on the delivery of their goods. Their valuable goods betrayed their wealth and they were killed, dismembered, and pickled for sale. The sorrowful Nicholas saw all this in a vision and confronted the murdering innkeeper. Nicholas prayed and obtained divine intercession, after which, the boys were miraculously reassembled, emerged from the pickling vat and went off to study. Well, how can they resume their studies after such an ordeal? We think they went off and really got properly pickled.

Table 1: Saints and their conceits or symbols

234

SYMBOL	MEANING
Anchor	faith and belief
Clover	Trinity
Column	crucifixion
Coral	protection against evil spirits
Dove	Holy Spirit (John 1:32), annunciation
Finch	shown with thorn in beak – passion
Fish*	generic Christian symbol
Grapes*	Eucharistic wine
Ladder	crucifixion
Lamb	Christ (John 1:29)
Lance	crucifixion
Lily	purity of Mary; symbol of Joseph
Nimbus (round halo)	dead holy person
Nimbus (square)	living holy person
Palm frond	martyrdom
Pelican	Christ
Pomegranate	fertility and rebirth
Ribbon or rope	Assumption of Mary
Ship	the Church
Sponge	crucifixion
Wheat	Eucharistic bread

Table 2. **Church Iconography and meaning**

*Christianity does not have a monopoly on some symbols. Visit a medieval Jewish cemetery and you will see tombstones with two hands (Cohanim-descendants of a priest), fish (death in the month of Adar), grapes (symbol of Israel), wolf (tribe of Benjamin), etc. These two examples come from the Jewish cemetery in Prague (AP).

Divine Loves of Zeus

Aphrodite:	Goddess of Love, accursed by Hera (Zeus' legit wife).
Asteria:	Assumed many forms to evade Zeus, ultimately flew from heaven as a quail into the Aegean Sea where she became Delos.
Demeter:	Goddess of Agriculture who mated with Zeus as entwined serpents giving birth to Persephone.
Dione:	Referred to as the mother of Aphrodite or Venus.
Eurynome:	By Zeus gave birth to the three Graces (Kharites).
Gaia:	Goddess of earth who with Zeus birthed Agdistis in Phrygia and Kypris in Cyprus.
Hera:	Queen of the gods who wed Zeus and gave him divine children – Ares, Eileithyia, Eris, Hephaestus and Hebe. Frequently furious at Zeus' indiscretions, she took imaginative revenges on some of his conquests.
Hybris:	Goddess of Pride – some say she gave birth to Pan through Zeus.
Kalliope:	Goddess of Music and one of the nine muses.
Leto:	Through Zeus bore the twin gods Apollo and Artemis.
Metis:	Zeus impregnated her, then learned the oracle that she would bear a son greater than he, so Zeus swallowed her. It was all for naught, because she gave birth to Athena.
Mnemosyne:	Disguised as a shepherd, Zeus spent nine nights with her and she gave birth to the nine muses.
Nemesis:	Goddess of retribution who shares the same fate as Leda.
Persephone:	(Oh, there's a lot of incest here) Goddess of Spring seduced by Zeus as a snake. When she was demoted to goddess of the underworld Zeus disguised himself as Hades and again fooled around with her.
Selene:	Goddess of the moon who bore Zeus daughters Pandia and Ersa.
Styx:	Goddess of the river Styx.
Themis:	Bore Zeus the three Horai, goddesses of the seasons and the three Morai or Fates.

Nymph Loves of Zeus

Aigina:	Zeus assumed the guise of an eagle and flew off with her to the Island of Aigina.
Aix:	Wife of Pan, turned herself into a goat to escape Zeus; it didn't turn Zeus off and she bore him a son named Aigipan.
Maia:	Nymph of Arcadia who gave birth to Hermes.
Nymph Africanus:	A Moor and mother of Iarbos by Zeus.
Nymph Sithnis:	Was the mother of Megaros by Zeus.
Nymph Samothrake:	Look, let us just assume from here on in that these seductions will all result in a little or minor god or goddess – except for Hermes of course.
Othreis:	ditto
Plouto:	ditto
Sinope:	Abducted to Assyria, Zeus promised her a wish. She said, "I wish to remain a virgin." Oi, that'll teach him
Taygete:	ditto

Mortal Loves of Zeus

Alkmene:	Zeus assumed the guise of her husband and had her and she gave him Herakles.
Antiope:	Zeus assumed the guise of Satyros. She bore twins then exposed them.
Danaë:	Zeus as a shower of gold, impregnated her, and she gave birth to Perseus.
Elare:	love of Zeus, she feared Hera's wrath, so she hid under the earth.
Europa:	Zeus as a bull, carried her off to Crete.
Eurymedousa:	Zeus made her an ant (why?), then made love to her (and an ant-man, Myrmidon, resulted).
Ganymedes:	Here's a switch. Zeus thought him lovely and in the guise of an eagle abducted him to Olympos to be his lover and cupbearer.
Kallisto:	Zeus seduced her. When Artemis got wind of this, she turned Kallisto into a bear and set loose her dogs. Zeus rescued her and put her in the heavens as Ursa major, with her son as Ursa minor.
Kalyke:	Gave birth to Endymion.

237

Kassiopeia:	Also made it to the heavens.
Lamia:	From Lybia. Hera was jealous and stole her children.
Laodameia:	daughter of Bellerophon and Philonoe and the mother of Sarpedon by Zeus. She was shot by Artemis when she was weaving.
Leda:	Seduced by Zeus who had become a swan, and she produced two very fertile eggs.
Lysithoe:	mother of Helenus by Zeus
Niobe:	The first mortal loved by Zeus who produced Argos and Pelasgos.
Olympias:	Mother of Alexander the Great.
Pandora:	First human created by the gods Hephaestus and Athena as instructed by Zeus, but of notoriety because of the jar she opened.
Pyrrha:	daughter of Epimetheus and Pandora and wife of Deucalion. When Zeus ended the Bronze Age with the great deluge, Deucalion and his wife, Pyrrha, were the only survivors.
Phthia:	Zeus assumed the guise of a dove … and ditto
Semela:	Now this is interesting. Jealous Hera rigged the thunder bolts of Zeus which had the effect of melting Semela. Zeus rescued their unborn son, Dionysos, sewed him up in his thigh until mature enough to be born. Wow! Short-circuitry and transplantation – basic science.
Thyia:	with Zeus bore Delphos

Table 3. **Loves of Zeus (courtesy of Theoi Greek Mythology)**

MAJOR GODS

GREEK	ROMAN	OLYPMPIAN SYMBOLS
Aphrodite	Venus	mirror, dove, rose, pomegranate
Apollo	Apollo	sun, lyre, chariot
Ares	Mars	helmet, armor
Artemis	Diana	bow and arrows, crescent moon
Athena	Minerva	helmet, owl, spear Aegis (shield)
Demeter	Ceres	cornucopia, sickle, wheat
Dionysus	Bacchus	grapevine, cup, thyrsus (fennel)
Hades	Pluto	owl, helm of darkness
Hephaestus	Vulcan	anvil, hammer
Hera	Juno	cow, peacock, diadem
Hermes	Mercury	winged sandals/cap, caduceus
Hestia	Vesta	fire, hearth, altar
Leto	Latona	spindle, veil, dates
Poseidon	Neptune	trident, dolphin
Zeus	Jupiter	eagle, thunderbolt, Aegis

MINOR GODS

Boreas*	Septentrio	winter, north wind
Eris	Discordia	golden apple
Eros	Cupid	bow and arrows, heart, wings
Hebe	Juventus	cupbearer
Hecate	Trivia	torch, dagger
Hypnos	Somnus	poppy
Iris	Arcus	rainbow, fleur-de-lis
None	Janus	door, key
Morpheus	Insomnia	closed eye
Nemesis	Nemesis	scales, broken wheel
Nyx	Nox	black star, crescent
Pan	Faunus	syrinx (panpipes)
Persephone	Proserpina	grain, pomegranate
Thanatos	Letus	Theta, extinguished torch
Tyche	Fortuna	cornucopia, wheel of fortune

Table 4. **Symbols of the gods**

---

*One of the four winds, the Anemoi. The other three were Zephyrus (west and spring), Notos (south and summer) and Eurus (east and sirocco).

SYMBOL	MEANING
Acorn	God's creation, human potential
Apple	original sin
Birds, nautilus-the exotic	luxury, wealth
Books	knowledge
Bread	humility, bread of life – communion host
Bubbles	transience of life
Butter	excess to encourage moderation
Candle	transience of life
Carpet	wealth
Cat	unteachable
Cherries	fruit of paradise
Chestnuts	triumph over temptation
Dog	fidelity
Dolphin	friendship, exploration
Flower petals	transience of life
Fruit basket	fertility
Glass	fragility, transience of life
Gold or silver	wealth
Goose	gluttony
Grapes	wine
Herring	humility
Hourglass, butterfly	transience of life
Iris	3 petals - Trinity
Jewels	wealth and power
Ledger book	trade and wealth
Maps	exploration, trade, wealth
Meats, ham, game	temptation, transience of life
Musical instruments	earthly delights, warnings about luxury
Onions	humility
Oranges, lemons	luxury from trade
Oysters	aphrodisiac, temptation
Playing cards	earthly pleasures
Porcelain	wealth, luxury
Pretzel	sexual tension
Shells	exploration, pilgrimage
Skull	vanitas
Smoke	transience of life (Psalm 102:3)
Snails	humility
Sunshine	God or divine light
Violin	beware the sinful life
Walnuts	cross of Christ
Window – open	the world
Wine	wealth, blood of Christ

Table 5. **Dutch Iconographic Elements**

Table 6. **Adult Death Iconoclasses**
With some exceptions (underlined), these symbols were seldom used for children.

a) Classical / Allegorical Reformation	b) Medieval	c) Renaissance/
door	skeleton	mirror
curtain	*transi*	candle
urn	*ars moriendi*	smoke
chin-strap	*3Living-3Dead*	mourning child
mourning women	*Danse macabre*	spent torch / rocket
eidolon	*Triumphus mortis*	*Aetates hominis*
thread of life	skull / cross-bones	scythe / knife
pomegranate	hild as soul	*homo bulla*
poppies	hyena / vulture / raven	flowers
broken column	owl	butterfly
Nyx, Thanatos	kiss of death	glass globe
Charon	shadow of death	Terminus
Persephone	bell	withered tree
Kronos / Saturn	arrow	classical dress
Hermes / Mercury	spade	d) Eighteenth century
conclamatio / *prothesis*	hourglass	weeping willow
kline	measuring rod / staff	
	shroud	

241

Table 7. **Childhood Death Iconoclasses**

1) The child sarcophagus
    a) *conclamatio*
    b) biographical

2) The commemorative stele

    a) fruit
    b) pets
    c) toys
    d) bulla

3) Commemorative Greek pottery
    a) Charon
    b) *prothesis*

4) Commemorative painting
    a) Portraits
      i) clouds / heavenly ascent / angels
      ii) allegorical dress
      iii) closed eyes
      iv) butterflies / flowers / hourglass / torch
    b) Epitaph paintings
      i) hidden faces
      ii) pallor
      iii) head wreaths
    c) Family portraits
      i) pointing
      ii) grave robes / shrouds

5) Commemorative sculpture
    a) at prayer
    b) asleep
    c) at play

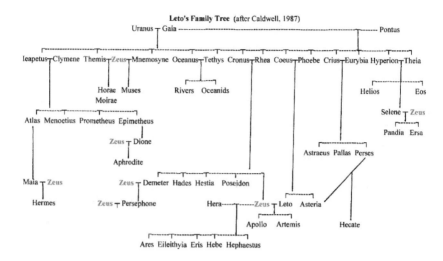

Leto's Family Tree (after Caldwell, 1987)

243